CHALLENGES ARE OPPORTUNITIES

Your Ultimate 'How-To' Manual for Crushing Obstacles and Launching Yourself Forward

SHAUN OLIVER

A FREE GIFT For You!

Download this **book** from our site:

Link: **selfhelppowers.com/resources/**

In **"21 Hacks of Motivation,"** delve into a treasure trove of strategies tailored to ignite your inner drive and propel you towards success.

With a keen understanding that motivation is not one-size-fits-all, this book offers a diverse array of twenty-one actionable hacks, each designed to resonate with different personalities, circumstances, and goals.

From time-tested techniques to cutting-edge insights, discover how to unlock your limitless potential, overcome obstacles, and craft a life fueled by unwavering determination.

GET IT FREE FOR A LIMITED TIME!

Copyright © 2024 by Shaun Oliver

All rights reserved. This book is protected by the copyright laws. This book may not be copied or reprinted for commercial gain or profit. The use of short quotations for reviews and articles is permitted. Permission will be granted upon request.

The reader of this publication assumes responsibility for the use of the information in this book. The author and publisher assume no responsibility or liability whatsoever on the behalf of the reader of this publication.

While efforts have been made to verify information and use accurate information, neither the author nor the publisher make any warranties with respect to errors, inaccuracies, or omissions.

For more information, visit: **selfhelppowers.com**

CONTENTS
CHALLENGES ARE OPPORTUNITIES

- CHAPTER 1 6
  - An Introduction to Challenges and Opportunities 6
- CHAPTER 2 23
  - Background of Challenges 23
- CHAPTER 3 38
  - Positive Mind System 38
- CHAPTER 4 57
  - Your Winning Strategy 57
- CHAPTER 5 70
  - Success In Professional Life..70
- CHAPTER 6 84
  - Success In Personal Life 84
- CHAPTER 7 114
  - Your Complete Security System..114
- CHAPTER 8 123
  - A Look at The Important Points 123
- BONUS CHAPTER..136
- ABOUT THE AUTHOR...140

CHAPTER 1
An Introduction to Challenges and Opportunities

It was a time of success and growing power for America in global trade. The stock market was on an all-time high like never before. Investors, hungry for chances and growth, gladly boosted it since 1923. Yet, life sometimes throws curveballs. Slowly but surely, a feeling of unease crept into the market. This was either unknown to those passionately hunting for progress, or maybe they just brushed it aside as a slight chance of a market drop.

The year 1929 arrived with a contrasting atmosphere. On October 24, a staggering five billion dollars vanished from the market in a single day. The decline persisted on the following day and continued its relentless descent. Contrary to expectations of a market recovery, the downward spiral persisted, culminating in the fateful Black Tuesday, October 29, 1929. The New York Stock Exchange plummeted even further, losing a colossal $14 billion. This cataclysmic loss etched its place in history, forever synonymous with despair—'The Great Depression.'

Unquestionably, it was the most formidable economic depression in modern history, originating from the United States and rapidly spreading to major countries worldwide between 1930 and 1933. The ensuing recession plunged nations into an abyss of economic turmoil, grinding international trade to a halt and halting the wheels of industrial progress. Countless individuals lost their livelihoods, and the effects rippled across communities, affecting millions.

Estimates reveal that over 130 million individuals were left unemployed due to the Great Depression. Between 1929 and 1932, industrial production rates plummeted by a staggering 45 percent, while housing construction experienced a crippling decline of 80 percent. Agricultural production suffered a significant blow, dropping by as much as 60 percent.

The psychological impact of the stock market crash in the United States reverberated deeply, prompting a drastic reduction in expenditures. Individuals found themselves unable to repay loans to banks, leading to a wave of withdrawals from deposited funds. The banking system ground to a halt, resulting in the bankruptcy and closure of thousands of banks—over five thousand in total.

It took nearly a decade for the world to recover from the grips of this recession. In the face of such adversity, could there be any glimmer of hope for progress? Though challenging to fathom, even during those trying times, certain visionary entrepreneurs and companies managed to steer the treacherous landscape. Among them, a prominent name that thrived amidst the severe recession was none other than today's well-known enterprise, Procter & Gamble.

It is essential to dig into the remarkable story of Procter & Gamble, a company that not only weathered the storm of economic adversity but also emerged stronger than ever before. Established in 1837, Procter & Gamble's remarkable performance during that era continues to be the subject of awe-inspiring conversations to this day.

So, what was their secret? Procter & Gamble possessed a profound understanding that the products they crafted held immense value for people. In times of difficulty, individuals may cut back on various expenses, but their fundamental needs persistently take precedence. Even something as simple as soap became an indispensable necessity in the lives of many. They recognized the unwavering demand for their products, regardless of the recessionary challenges.

When a demand exists, it becomes crucial to bring it to the forefront of public consciousness. The most apparent solution? Advertising. However, during times of economic downturns, businesses often resort to slashing their advertising budgets as a means of cost-cutting. In such perplexing circumstances, a clear resolution seemed elusive.

In the world of marketing, a timeless saying remains: "Never forsake the very aspect of your business that attracts customers." Procter & Gamble wholeheartedly adopted this philosophy. They comprehended that ceasing advertising altogether was unnecessary, but rather, they needed to redirect their advertising investments toward initiatives that would yield the greatest returns.

In those bygone days, people remained connected to their radios even while engaged in mundane tasks. Radio serials were gaining immense popularity, capturing the attention of a vast audience. Sensing an opportunity, Procter & Gamble pioneered the art of sponsorship, forging connections with individuals through these engaging radio serials. This groundbreaking approach sought to establish an emotional bond with the audience, transcending the conventional boundaries of direct advertising.

By 1939, Procter & Gamble proudly sponsored an impressive roster of 21 radio shows. Additionally, during this time, they boldly ventured into the world of television commercials, further expanding their reach and impact. Engaging in various small-scale branding activities, they endeavored to connect with their customers on a personal level. Their initiatives even extended to the distribution of product samples, directly reaching out to potential consumers. Each product was carefully positioned as a distinct brand, fostering a genuine connection with the people they served.

The results speak volumes. Ninety years after this pivotal period, Procter & Gamble still stands tall, its legacy firmly entrenched in every household. While many businesses of that era have faded into obscurity, Procter & Gamble has left an indelible mark on the fabric of society, embodying resilience and unwavering success.

The Greatest Lesson from the Greatest Recession

The Great Depression of the 1930s stands as a painful chapter in history, but it was far from the end of the world. Rather, it marked the dawning of a new era. Amidst the turmoil, numerous entrepreneurs rose to unprecedented heights, achieving feats that surpassed all expectations. It was an era defined by perseverance, resilience, and remarkable accomplishments.

The Great Depression of the 1930s was not the first, nor the last, economic downturn to shake the world. Similar challenges unfolded in 1992 and 2008, and numerous smaller-scale recessions have occurred in different corners of the globe throughout history. Even the year 2020-21 presented its own unique set of trials, and it is conceivable that future challenges lie ahead.

Undoubtedly, challenges will arise, but the greater truth is that where challenges emerge, so do solutions. This is the fundamental law of creation, and it manifests itself in various forms and iterations.

Necessity has forever been the catalyst for invention, and emptiness has always been the fertile ground for creation. The world progresses through change, and each moment births new circumstances that lay the groundwork for future challenges. Thus, the question remains: should we fear these challenges, or should we confront them with unwavering courage? And if we choose to face them fearlessly, do we possess the necessary means to do so? The resounding answer is a simple "Yes." You possess the inherent capacity not only to steer through these challenges but also to transform them into unparalleled opportunities.

Every Challenge is an Unveiled Opportunity!

When faced with a daunting challenge, it is natural to feel overwhelmed. The enormity of the task at hand can obscure the hidden opportunity lying within. However, it is precisely during these moments that great courage is required to not only acknowledge the potential opportunity but also to seize it with unwavering determination.

Too often, when challenges arise, anxiety takes hold, clouding your vision and preventing you from recognizing the opportunities concealed within. Yet, with a shift in perspective and a willingness to adopt adversity, remarkable transformations can occur.

Let us explore more into the depths of history and draw inspiration from the Great Depression of 1930. During this tumultuous time, the world grappled with a severe economic recession that cast its shadow over nearly every nation. Businesses crumbled, debts multiplied, and ordinary individuals found themselves ensnared in a web of unprecedented challenges.

Amidst the chaos, there was an ordinary businessman who, like many others, faced the harsh reality of diminishing resources.

With a small sum of money remaining, he could have chosen the path of mere survival, living month to month, merely existing. However, deep within his soul, he knew that life was not meant to be merely endured but embraced.

Initially, frustration and anger consumed him, and he even directed his ire towards fate itself. But these futile outbursts yielded no solutions. In the depths of his disappointment, a seed of inspiration germinated within his mind. He pondered the possibility of transforming this challenge into an opportunity.

While others shied away from entrepreneurship, he recognized the void in the market and the unmet basic needs of the people. The absence of competition in this tumultuous era presented a unique advantage. With a surge of determination, he reinvested a significant portion of his remaining capital into his business.

To his astonishment, a series of extraordinary events unfolded. He swiftly hired a qualified salesman at a low salary, who, driven by the same spirit, started on delivering goods door-to-door. The unemployed youths, who languished on street corners, found purpose and income by becoming commission agents for his venture.

In the blink of an eye, his business regained momentum. The capital he had reinvested yielded manifold returns, opening new doors for further expansion. The dedicated salesman, who had initially accepted a modest wage, ascended the ranks as the business flourished.

In this remarkable transformation, the businessman discovered the profound truth that lies within every challenge—an opportunity eagerly waiting to be utilized. By viewing his predicament through the lens of possibility rather than adversity, he not only salvaged his business but also achieved unprecedented success. He is not a very famous personality, but one of those small winners who converted challenges into opportunities. He was my great grandfather who started his small textile business and flourished it to great heights. He supported not only his family but also the entire community.

Such stories of triumph abound in the world of business and in our everyday lives. Yet, how often do you pause to consider the challenges you face as potential gateways to unparalleled opportunities?

The Attitude that Sets the Tone

Life is like a big game. We find problems and solutions mixed together. Imagine if we changed how we see things. What if we found treasures in the mess? The right attitude is a magic key. It opens a door to so many chances we didn't see before.

Let me tell you another story. There was a major shoe company, where the owner aimed to broaden his business into uncharted territories. As he interviewed numerous candidates for the role of sales manager, he encountered individuals with impressive academic credentials and extensive experience. Yet, none of them resonated with the owner's vision.

In the midst of this process, a young boy entered the interview room. He lacked notable educational qualifications and had no prior experience in the field. However, his presence intrigued the owner, who decided to interview him.

To the astonishment of others, the owner appointed the young man as the sales manager. Curiosity and confusion engulfed the minds of those who questioned the owner's decision.

A few days later, the owner sent both the new sales manager and the old sales manager on a mission to explore new business opportunities in the interior of Africa. Within a week, the owner received emails from both individuals, each portraying a starkly contrasting outlook on their circumstances.

The old sales manager's email carried a tone of despair, stating that people in that region did not wear shoes, making any possibilities seem futile.

On the other hand, the email from the new sales manager emanated an aura of excitement and optimism. He recognized the lack of footwear as an extraordinary opportunity to establish the company's brand in an untapped market.

A smile gradually spread across the owner's face as he absorbed the contents of the emails. Summoning his colleagues, he shared the correspondence, proclaiming, "Now you understand why I chose this young man as our sales manager.

It is the power of perspective that sets him apart. This individual possesses an exceptional ability to perceive possibilities where others see obstacles. I firmly believe that such managers will propel us towards unparalleled success."

The owner's prophetic words soon came to fruition. Through astute branding and strategic marketing, the shoe company ventured into new territories that were once deemed impenetrable by competitors. They harnessed the untapped potential of a market where shoes were a rarity, transforming it into a playground of triumph and prosperity.

Attitude functions as your compass, directing your journey. When you look at situations through a distorted viewpoint, the path ahead remains concealed. Yet, by adopting the correct outlook, you can uncover possibilities within challenges, revealing the latent potential ready for you.

A Valuable Lesson from Nature

Have you ever found yourself complaining about the timing of difficulties or questioning why challenges arise at all? It's natural to attribute misfortunes to external factors such as timing or luck. However, let us pause and reflect on whether this perspective aligns with the teachings of nature. Does nature truly encourage us to avoid challenges?

I want to share a thought-provoking tale that sheds light on this concept. Once, a farmer grew increasingly frustrated with God. He experienced the unpredictable nature of farming firsthand—floods, droughts, scorching sun, and even hailstorms. Each time, some of his crops, whether in lesser or greater amounts, suffered ruin. Overwhelmed by his mounting troubles, the farmer summoned God, presenting his grievances. He candidly expressed, "Dear Lord, your divinity is unquestionable, but it appears that you lack an understanding of farming. Your assessment of suitable weather conditions for crops seems flawed. I beseech you, grant me control over the weather for a year, and witness how I fill the world with abundant harvests." Amused, God responded with a smile, saying, "Very well, the weather shall be as you desire. I shall not interfere."

The farmer proceeded to sow his wheat crop, enjoying the privilege of tailor-made conditions. Sunlight blessed the crop when needed, and water quenched its thirst without delay. Harsh sunlight, hail, floods, and storms were kept at bay. With time, the crop flourished, and the farmer beheld it with delight. Never before had he witnessed such a remarkable yield. Filled with self-assurance, he contemplated, "Finally, God will comprehend the art of farming. We farmers have endured countless hardships unnecessarily over the years."

When the time for harvesting arrived, the farmer eagerly ventured to reap the fruits of his labor. However, as he commenced the harvest, he abruptly halted, his hand resting on his chest in despair. To his dismay, every single ear of wheat was empty, completely devoid of grain. Overwhelmed by sadness, the farmer summoned God once again. God appeared, observing the farmer's deep disappointment. Puzzled, the farmer implored, "Dear Lord, what has befallen my crop? I ensured favorable conditions throughout the year, so why is the yield so futile?"

God replied, "It was inevitable. You denied the plants an opportunity to fight for their existence. They were shielded from basking in the scorching sun, spared the struggle against hailstorms, and deprived of any kind of challenge. Consequently, the plants grew but remained hollow within. When a storm arises, bringing heavy rain and hail, it is through their own resilience that plants withstand the adversity. The struggle to preserve their existence generates strength, energy, and vitality. Even gold must endure exposure to intense heat, undergo melting, and endure hammering to become precious. Only by undergoing such challenges does its golden aura emerge, rendering it invaluable. Likewise, a life devoid of struggle and challenges leaves an individual hollow, devoid of virtue. To develop strength and talent, one must forge ahead, perceiving challenges as opportunities."

The farmer grasped the essence of God's message and humbly folded his hands in reverence. He acknowledged, "Lord, I leave the task to you."

Therefore, even nature itself does not advocate evading challenges; rather, it presents them as opportunities for personal growth. By constantly evading challenges, you risk missing out on the invaluable gifts that nature offers. In doing so, challenges persist, obstructing your path, while the hidden opportunities within them remain unseen.

Importance of challenges in life

Challenges are an integral part of life, and they play a crucial role in shaping who you are. In fact, without challenges, the very essence and purpose of life would lose its meaning. It is through challenges that you discover your true potential and maintain a sense of vitality and enthusiasm towards life.

Let me share another intriguing story to illustrate the significance of challenges. In a small country, the inhabitants had an insatiable appetite for fresh sea fish. However, due to the scarcity of nearby water sources, obtaining fresh fish posed a great challenge. To meet the people's demand, fishing boats began to increase in number and size, aiming to bring in more fish with each trip. These boats ventured far and wide in search of fresh catch. While they were successful in bringing back a larger quantity of fish, the extended journeys took a toll on the fish's freshness, compromising their taste.

To address this issue, fishing companies equipped their boats with freezers. The fish caught were immediately frozen, allowing the boats to start on longer expeditions and stay at sea for extended periods. However, the frozen fish failed to impress the consumers, who could discern the disparity in taste between fresh and frozen fish. Consequently, the frozen catch started to fetch lower prices.

Undeterred by this setback, the fishing companies devised a new strategy by installing fish tanks directly on their boats. They would catch the fish and place them in these tanks, providing them with nourishment. Initially, the fish displayed some activity, but soon their movements became sluggish after being satiated. While the fish remained alive during the journey, their lack of vitality and freshness became evident upon arrival. People continued to prefer the vibrant taste of truly fresh fish.

The fishing companies pondered over this persistent challenge, seeking a solution that would restore the desired taste and freshness. Finally, they identified the key to their predicament: challenges.

This time, they maintained the fish tanks as before, providing regular sustenance to the fish. However, they introduced a small shark into the tank. As soon as the fish entered the tank, they were confronted with the challenge of coexisting with the shark. Constantly alert and engaged, the fish had to steer their way around this formidable adversary. While some fish fell victim to the shark, the majority managed to survive. When people savored these fish, they were captivated by the authentic taste of freshness. They marveled at the liveliness preserved within the fish.

The fish's journey demonstrates a valuable lesson imparted by nature. Throughout human civilization, it has been observed that cultures and societies that faced and overcame challenges emerged stronger and more resilient. Conversely, civilizations built without encountering significant challenges have faded into oblivion, leaving no trace behind.

Benefits of challenges in life

As you relentlessly pursue progress, remember that the challenges you face often hold hidden treasures waiting to be discovered. While losses and setbacks may occupy your thoughts, it is crucial to recognize the countless benefits that challenges bring into your life. Let's explore some of these transformative advantages:

1. Challenges make you realize how strong you are.

True strength reveals itself when the circumstances demand it. Just as muscles grow and strengthen through resistance training, life requires challenges to foster growth and improvement. Each challenge you face serves as an opportunity to enhance your resilience. Accept them, for they are the true litmus test of your capabilities. In ordinary times, anyone can claim strength, but it is during challenges that the mighty are truly distinguished.

2. Challenges foster gratitude.

Amidst challenging times, fear of losing what you hold dear may arise, but it is during these moments that you also recognize the inherent value of what you possess. You might find that you often overlook the simple and natural blessings around you until they become endangered. It's during times of adversity and loss that you can develop a stronger sense of gratitude and cultivate compassion for those around you. Challenges evoke positive emotions and dismantle negative ones like ego and fear.

3. Challenges illuminate your life's true purpose.

During times of routine and normalcy, it is easy to lose sight of your genuine desires and aspirations. However, when faced with challenges, you are presented with an opportunity to reflect upon your life and discern your true calling. For instance, being stuck in a monotonous job may blind you to your life's purpose. Yet, when faced with job-related problems and discontent, you begin to question and uncover your authentic path. Welcome challenges as catalysts for introspection and gain clarity on your goals. With newfound clarity, you can march forward with diligence towards realizing your dreams.

4. Challenges cultivate determination and patience.

Emerging from a storm, you are no longer the person who entered it; you transform into something greater. Many successful individuals credit their resilience and tenacity as fundamental pillars of their achievements. Rather than perceiving defeat and challenges as obstacles, they perceive past failures as fuel that propels them towards success. Those who shun challenges miss out on the valuable lessons of overcoming adversity, developing character, and formulating effective strategies for triumph. Challenges grant you the capability to confront future obstacles with unwavering determination, while those who avoid challenges succumb to fear even in the face of minor predicaments.

5. Challenges ignite your creativity.

Challenges serve as catalysts for unlocking your creative prowess. The most arduous circumstances often demand the most innovative solutions. Scientists have made groundbreaking discoveries in response to challenges, and ingenious systems are devised to tackle adversity. Remarkably, even in the face of daunting challenges, individuals showcase extraordinary creativity by devising unconventional solutions. These creative breakthroughs are born out of the necessity to conquer challenges.

6. Challenges infuse meaning into your achievements.

Success that follows arduous struggles and defeats tastes sweeter. You have likely experienced this firsthand. The elation derived from conquering challenges is unparalleled. In essence, challenges redefine success. It's important to remember that success is not merely a destination; it's an ongoing journey. The richness and allure of this journey lie within the challenges you encounter. The value of your accomplishments is magnified when you have overcome numerous obstacles to reach your goals. Some achievements may lose their luster if they were attained without facing significant challenges.

Upon closer examination, every challenge carries within it a multitude of opportunities. These opportunities, intertwined with challenges, awaken your latent potential, fortify your character, instill humility, and lend true meaning to your accomplishments. Accept challenges as the stepping stones to your personal growth and success. Through challenges, you will unearth a reservoir of strength and resilience that you never knew existed within you. Welcome them as transformative gifts that propel you towards your highest potential.

Turning Challenges into Opportunities: Unveiling a System for Success

Life is filled with challenges, from global economic recessions to everyday struggles faced by ordinary individuals. The question arises: how can you confront these challenges and emerge stronger? It is crucial to recognize that challenges are an inherent part of your existence, and as long as the world persists, they will persist as well. However, there exists a remarkable system—a system that can transform challenges into opportunities, empowering you to achieve success despite the obstacles. The purpose of this book is to introduce you to this extraordinary system and guide you on a transformative journey. Let's have a glance at chapters:

Within the pages of this book, I will provide a comprehensive explanation of this transformative system. To enhance clarity, the book is divided into eight main parts, with a deliberate focus on the solution rather than dwelling excessively on the problems themselves. The initial section aims to equip you with practical insights, setting the stage for your transformative journey.

In the second part of the book, we dig into the most effective approach for problem-solving—the root-cause analysis. This chapter holds paramount significance, not only offering techniques to tackle challenges but also serving as the key to unlocking your victory. It is akin to a door through which the light of hope will shine brightly.

The third part of the book centers on the mindset necessary to confront challenges and view them as opportunities. While the importance of a positive mindset is widely acknowledged, only a few possess the knowledge of applying it practically during challenging times. This chapter provides practical methods to empower you with the mindset required to steer obstacles successfully.

The fourth part of the book propels you into action. Regardless of your current circumstances, this chapter presents detailed insights into initiating immediate positive changes in your life. It provides a roadmap to creating a personal system that transforms every challenge into an opportunity.

The fifth part of the book assumes paramount importance, addressing the challenges faced in your professional life and transforming them into opportunities. This chapter lays the foundation for your success, offering solutions not only for current hurdles but also for securing a better future.

In the sixth part of the book, we explore the challenges of personal life and how these challenges can be transformed into opportunities. By implementing the strategies and techniques outlined, you can cultivate a life filled with positivity and growth.

Upon reaching the seventh part, you will have become intimately acquainted with the system. However, understanding the system alone is insufficient; it is essential to ensure its smooth operation and sustained continuity. This chapter presents an incredible method through which you can guarantee your ongoing success.

The final part of the book serves as a concise summary, highlighting the key points of the system in a straightforward manner. This summary will enable you to grasp the essential principles and actively apply them, thereby positively changing your life.

Next Step

Begin a remarkable journey as I introduce you to an exceptional system—a system that can transform every challenge into an opportunity. Equipped with the knowledge and tools provided within this book, you will be empowered to face any obstacle with resilience and unlock the path to personal and professional success. Let us get on this transformative journey together and witness the incredible possibilities that await you!

CHAPTER 2
Background of Challenges

In a faraway kingdom, a wise and kind king ruled his land. His rule was marked by prosperity and harmony, as the kingdom flourished under his guidance. However, as the king advanced in age, a newfound concern for his subjects began to stir within his heart. He pondered deeply, questioning whether his subjects truly understood their responsibilities, possessed unwavering respect for human values, and possessed the mindset necessary to overcome challenges. The king realized that he could not always lead his people directly. In the face of adversity, it was their values and mindset that would pave the way for progress.

With the intention of gauging the determination and resilience of his subjects, the king devised a plan. Early the next morning, a large stone was strategically placed on the main road of the kingdom. Concealing himself with a few trusted companions, the king observed the unfolding scene.

Slowly, the road filled with people starting their everyday trips. Everyone encountered difficulty upon noticing the stone obstructing the path. Some individuals hurriedly maneuvered around it, seeking to avoid any inconvenience. Others directed their anger toward an unknown culprit responsible for leaving the stone in their way. A few even went so far as to curse the government for its apparent negligence in maintaining clean roads.

State ministers and affluent individuals also crossed the road, yet they too chose to sidestep the stone, uttering complaints under their breath. The diverse reactions of the people surprised the king greatly, leaving him disheartened by the perceived deviation from cherished values. However, the king did not lose hope entirely. He continued to observe the road, yearning for a glimmer of resilience.

After some time, a humble farmer appeared on the road, balancing a basket laden with fresh vegetables upon his head. As he approached the stone, he noticed the obstruction. Although he could have easily circumvented it, the thought of ignoring the challenge never crossed his mind. Determined, he gingerly placed his vegetable-laden basket to the side and began exerting all his strength to dislodge the stone. Passersby witnessed his earnest efforts but chose to ridicule him instead of lending a helping hand. Undeterred by the laughter and dismissive comments, the farmer persevered.

Finally, the fruits of the farmer's labor became evident, as the stone was successfully moved from its entrenched position. To his astonishment, the farmer discovered a bag lying beneath the stone. With a mixture of curiosity and excitement, he opened the bag to reveal its gleaming contents—golden coins. A small slip of paper lay nestled within the bag. Upon unfolding it, the farmer's eyes scanned the words inscribed upon it: "Reward from the king to the one who removes the stone."

Overwhelmed with sheer joy, the farmer's heart brimmed with gratitude toward both the king and the divine. He collected the bag of riches, expressing his gratitude silently, and resumed his journey with the vegetable basket upon his head.

Witnessing this remarkable display of resilience, the king's faith in his subjects was rekindled. He understood that there were individuals who remained steadfast in their commitment to upholding values. As long as there existed tenacious souls like the hardworking farmer, those who refused to shy away from challenges but instead confronted them head-on, the golden gift of opportunity would forever be concealed within every trial.

Why do challenges bother you?

Have you ever wondered why challenges tend to rattle your nerves? Why do they have the power to make you feel uncomfortable and unsettled, regardless of their magnitude? The truth is, challenges are an inherent part of life—they manifest themselves in every age, at every stage. Life, when examined closely, can be likened to an embroidery woven with stories of overcoming challenges. Reflect upon your own life, and you'll discover that the most remarkable chapters are often those that emerged from navigating and conquering adversities.

In essence, challenges propel our lives forward. They serve as catalysts for growth and transformation. Yet, despite their undeniable significance, why do so many individuals struggle to face challenges with the right mindset? Why do challenges have the power to unsettle and disrupt our equilibrium?

It is undeniable that challenges exist in the present, and they will continue to shape our future. However, it is possible for these challenges to cease being a source of distress. You have the ability to cultivate a mindset that renders challenges inconsequential, unable to break your spirit.

Every challenge that comes your way holds the potential to become an opportunity—a stepping stone toward your desired destination. There exists a framework, a system, through which challenges can be seamlessly transformed into opportunities. But before delving into this system, it is imperative to comprehend why challenges tend to unsettle you in the first place.

The discomfort you experience when faced with challenges can be traced back to a fundamental aspect of human psychology—a deep-seated instinct for security. Since the dawn of humankind, the pursuit of security has been an intrinsic part of our nature. Our ancestors sought safety in numbers, forming tribes and communities. By banding together, they felt a sense of protection and security. To fortify this sense of security, individuals strove to attain financial stability, strengthen social bonds, establish religions, erect nations, and construct institutions. This quest for security persists to this day, deeply ingrained in our collective consciousness.

From a psychological standpoint, human security can be defined as "freedom from fear." It serves as a fundamental precondition for human progress. Development, in its true essence, aims to ensure that individuals have the freedom to lead long and healthy lives, acquire knowledge and education, and access resources that enhance their standard of living, fostering material progress.

So, why does this pursuit of security have an impact on your perception of challenges? It lies in the subconscious association of challenges with potential threats to your security and well-being. Your mind, wired for self-preservation, views challenges as obstacles that may disrupt the stability and comfort you have diligently cultivated.

However, it is crucial to recognize that this association between challenges and security is not an immutable truth. It is a conditioned response, a deeply ingrained belief system. By understanding the roots of this psychological tendency, you gain the power to transcend it. You can reframe your perception of challenges, shifting from a state of apprehension to one of empowerment.

If you have dived into the profound insights of renowned psychologist Maslow, you are already acquainted with the concept of human needs. Maslow's theory classifies needs into five distinct categories, each building upon the fulfillment of the previous one. Imagine it as a ladder or a pyramid, unfolding from the foundation to the pinnacle of self-actualization. Let's explore these five dimensions of needs.

First, we have physiological needs—the basic requirements for sustaining human life. These encompass essentials such as nourishment, water, shelter, sleep, and satisfying our primal instincts.

Once these physiological needs are met, the focus shifts to the second category—security needs. This encompasses the desire for physical, economic, and psychological security. Physical security entails safeguarding oneself from accidents, assaults, illnesses, and other unforeseen events. Economic security involves aspects such as stable employment and provisions for the future. Psychological security revolves around the need for justice, empathy, and liberation from uncertainty.

Moving up the ladder, we encounter the third set of needs—social affiliation. This encompasses the innate human yearning for belongingness, love, and connection.

Following this, we reach the fourth category—esteem needs. At this stage, individuals strive for recognition, respect, and a sense of significance.

Lastly, we ascend to the world of self-actualization needs. These needs arise from the aspiration to unleash one's full potential and start on a journey of personal growth and self-discovery.

Maslow's theory extends from the foundation of primary security to the pinnacle of spiritual fulfillment. You may wonder how this relates to challenges. In simple terms, anything that poses a threat to our sense of security or encroaches upon our comfort zone appears as a challenge. It is natural for individuals to experience distress and perceive such disruptions as obstacles.

Also, humans possess an inherent resistance to change. Often, we question the need for alteration when things seem to be going well. However, change is an immutable law of the universe. Every moment, every second, the world undergoes transformation. Without change, progress would grind to a halt. Therefore, it becomes crucial to confront the fear of change and view it not as a challenge, but as an opportunity for growth.

Now, as you reflect upon these insights, consider the impact they hold for your own life. Understand that challenges are not adversaries; they are catalysts for transformation. They have the power to propel you towards reaching your fullest potential.

Navigating Challenges of Life

In the journey of life, challenges unfurl in various forms and at different junctures. Broadly speaking, challenges can be categorized into five distinct domains. Let us explore these domains together and uncover the transformative opportunities they hold:

1. Personal Challenges:

At different stages of life, personal challenges may arise, often stemming from deep-rooted fears or self-perceived limitations. Some individuals carry unknown fears within them, hindering their progress. Additionally, the fear of failure, the fear of inadequacy, and the fear of inferiority can emerge as formidable challenges. A lack of self-belief or comparing oneself unfavorably to others may also contribute to these internal obstacles.

2. Emotional Challenges:

Emotional challenges often arise as an extension of personal struggles. Intense attachments to certain people, relationships, or possessions can transform even minor setbacks into significant challenges. In modern times, conflicts and fissures within relationships have become commonplace. Romantic relationships may experience distance or dissolution, while challenges between parents and children in building strong connections can surface. Likewise, disharmony with friends, colleagues, or associates can pose emotional challenges. The loss of a loved one can also plunge individuals into profound grief, creating enduring emotional obstacles.

3. Health Challenges:

In the contemporary era, health-related challenges have become increasingly prevalent. Neglecting one's well-being can lead to various health challenges as we age. Some health concerns are transient, such as fleeting fevers or colds that resolve over time. However, others, like chronic conditions such as diabetes or heart disease, persist as enduring challenges. Also, sudden accidents resulting in physical injuries can also give rise to health challenges that require attention and care.

4. Financial Challenges:

Financial challenges are often acknowledged as the most tangible and pressing obstacles. When discussing their challenges, many individuals predominantly cite financial difficulties. These challenges may arise due to various circumstances. Some may struggle to find stable employment, while others may earn a substantial income but struggle with financial mismanagement. Poor spending habits or unwise investments can lead to financial challenges. Moreover, business owners face the cyclical nature of ups and downs, and when the downs become overwhelming, significant financial challenges can ensue.

5. Unforeseen Challenges:

Unforeseen challenges hold a distinct place within the spectrum of life's trials. Unlike the previous four categories, you have limited or no direct control over these challenges. They often emerge abruptly, catching us off guard. For instance, sudden wartime situations can cripple economies, causing widespread upheaval. Global recessions, akin to the one experienced in the 1930s, can cast a shadow over the world. Similarly, pandemics such as the unprecedented COVID-19 outbreak in 2020 can disrupt societies worldwide. Unforeseen challenges have a cascading effect, often opening doors to additional types of challenges.

Is being upset the solution?

In life, challenges manifest in various forms, constantly ebbing and flowing. But let me ask you this: Is succumbing to fear the solution? Does becoming perturbed by these challenges serve any purpose? Absolutely not. Allowing yourself to be consumed by worry or anxiety is far from a solution. In fact, persisting in such a state for an extended period can lead to a multitude of additional problems.

Unceasing turmoil is the breeding ground for depression, which casts its shadow not only over your mental well-being but also affects your personal and professional life. The financial challenges that emerged in 2020 amidst the global pandemic exemplify this. The ripple effect of recession severely impacted people's mental health. Prolonged mental distress often spirals into deep-seated depression, bringing with it a myriad of consequences, even pushing some to the brink of despair.

Stress, in essence, is a form of mental helplessness. When you find yourself frustrated with a situation, feeling incapable of conquering the battle or succumbing to loneliness, it is within this helplessness that mental fatigue takes root. This fatigue lingers, and it is from here that the seeds of depression begin to sprout. Psychologists assert that if the situation shows no signs of improvement in the near future, mental health problems can escalate, increasing the risk of suicidal tendencies.

If one's inner strength is not fortified, stress can take hold in seemingly stress-free circumstances. For instance, when a person fails to achieve results commensurate with their abilities, their self-confidence starts to waver. Often, they perceive the pressures faced by their colleagues as personal burdens. Even the mildest criticism becomes distressing, triggering recurring episodes of stress.

Persistent stress begets a plethora of issues. Those affected struggle to sleep soundly, plagued by mental exhaustion. Unexplained surges of negative emotions course through their minds, causing sadness or anxiety even without a discernible cause. They find themselves caught in the grip of these negative emotions, unable to pinpoint the reason behind their distress.

Under the weight of stress, emotional comprehension deteriorates, leaving individuals unable to fully appreciate the present joys in life. Even amidst happiness, their minds harbor an underlying worry, fearing that it, too, will be snatched away. They remain ensnared in worries about the past and anxieties about the future, even during moments of celebration.

Experts identify nervousness, fear of infection, incessant restlessness, constant seeking of reassurance, sleep disturbances, excessive worrying, feelings of helplessness, and fear of financial loss as primary factors contributing to depression and anxiety. Concerns about job security, financial burdens, uncertainties about the future, and apprehensions about running out of essential resources exacerbate these issues.

The world around us is in constant flux, and change is an inevitability. What truly matters is how deeply it affects your inner being. Some individuals suddenly find themselves engulfed in negative emotions. They strive to cultivate positivity, yet these feelings persist. If you experience such negative emotions from time to time, it is an indication of stress. It is essential to steer these emotions through a proper process. Failing to do so allows tension to fester, ultimately transforming into depression, a formidable adversary that becomes increasingly difficult to overcome.

Extension of stress: more side effects

When challenges burden you with stress, it not only affects you but also casts a shadow over those around you. A single individual's stress can permeate an entire family, creating an atmosphere of tension that engulfs everyone. If that individual happens to be the head of the family, the gravity of the problem intensifies. Other family members bear the brunt of this stress, and the prospects of improving the situation dwindle.

Similarly, if you hold a leadership position or own a business, your stress can permeate your entire organization or team. The mood of a troubled leader becomes the mood of the entire team. If the leader remains in a state of perpetual tension, the team cohesion disintegrates.

Indeed, there are few individuals in this world who can truly thrive amidst challenging times, becoming a beacon of success. It holds true that one who can manage oneself can effectively manage other aspects of life. It all begins with self-management.

However, being plagued by challenges is far from a solution. If trouble befalls you, it should be addressed promptly. Allowing it to persist will only give rise to further complications.

The Solution Paths

So, you may wonder, is there a solution? Could you have taken preventive measures in the past to avert the current predicament? Or should you simply hope for things to improve spontaneously in the future? In reality, both of these approaches are misguided. The path to a solution lies neither in the sorrows of the past nor in the anxieties of the future. The real solution resides in the present moment.

If anything holds true in this world, it is the present moment in which you exist. There is no time before it, and there will be no time after it. The present is everything you have. Therefore, your focus should primarily be on the present, relinquishing concerns about both the past and the future. Worrying about what should have happened or what will happen is futile. Your actions today will become the past tomorrow, and the foundation for your future will be laid based on what you do in the present. In essence, all solutions lie within the present.

Living in the present moment is the key mantra for life. Practically speaking, whatever lies before you today, whether it be work responsibilities or familial duties, your utmost effort should be directed towards fulfilling them well, starting now. Similarly, when you are engaged in work, let your focus be solely on the task at hand. By setting aside other worries and concentrating on the present moment, you will experience a positive shift in your life.

The truth of life resides in the present. Therefore, you mustn't allow your thoughts to wander aimlessly between the past and the future. Your consciousness must be anchored in the present moment. Whenever your mind begins to stray, gently pull your thoughts back to the present. Initially, this may prove challenging, but with conscious effort, it will gradually become easier.

Recognize that the truth lies in what lies before you and it is your responsibility to steer it skillfully. Those who comprehend this responsibility and are able to fulfill it discover a natural equilibrium in their lives, where tension dissipates. Remember, the power to shape your reality lies in your hands, here and now.

Harnessing the Power of the Present

Life is all about the present. The past, with its wealth of experiences, serves as a guide to steer the present more efficiently. Similarly, thoughts of the future offer utility in planning your actions in the present. However, a mind consumed by either the past or the future finds it arduous to give undivided attention to the present. Emotional turmoil mounts to such an extent that it becomes challenging to maintain focus on the here and now.

It is imperative that you live in the present moment. Direct your focus towards what is achievable in the here and now. Contemplating both the past and the future is not detrimental, as long as their boundaries remain aligned with the present. Strive to make the most of today's possibilities. It is here that your intelligence and awareness should converge.

I share a story that encapsulates the essence of living in the present. Once, an old man was seated on an airplane when a young man took the seat beside him. The young man greeted the old man with a warm smile and eventually asked, "Sir, may I know the time in your watch?" The old man fell silent for a moment, then replied,

"I'm sorry, but I cannot tell you the time." Puzzled, the young man inquired, "Is your watch not functioning properly?"

The old man gently responded, "The watch is indeed functional and keeps ticking. However, if I were to reveal the time, it would initiate a conversation. You would ask me where I am headed, to which I would reply, 'New York.' In turn, you might disclose that you are also bound for the same destination. Curiosity would lead you to ask about my neighborhood, and reluctantly, I would divulge that if you ever visit, you are welcome at my place. Now, my daughter is young and beautiful. Undoubtedly, you would be attracted to her and suggest going to the movies together. She would agree, and this series of events might culminate in me contemplating whether or not to give my daughter's hand in marriage to you. Frankly, you don't strike me as the right match, so I kindly request that you refrain from asking for the time."

You may find amusement in this tale, but if you observe closely, you will realize that a significant portion of humanity follows a similar pattern. Lost in the mirage of the future, they become entangled in worries that never materialize. Being aware that these imagined future scenarios lack true substance breeds anxiety.

Often, people find themselves unable to fully adopt the present moment. They leapfrog between the future and the past, unable to remain anchored in the present, caught in needless concerns. However, both the future and the past are mere illusions of time. The only temporal reality is the present moment.

To truly thrive, it is crucial to focus on the present. Release the regrets of the past and liberate yourself from the unfounded worries about a future that is yet to unfold.

Regardless of the magnitude of the challenge you face, its solution resides in the present moment itself. This is an unwavering mantra, discovered through deep exploration of challenges.

Therefore, for now, hold steadfast to this powerful mantra: "The solution lies in the present."

Whatever happens, happens for the good!

No matter what circumstances unfold in your life, remember that they are all part of a grand plan for your greater good. At times, it may be challenging to accept unfavorable events, but in hindsight, you realize that those very experiences pave the way for remarkable blessings to enter your life.

I share an inspiring tale that has captured the hearts of many. Once, in a kingdom, there reigned a king whose minister was known for his unwavering positivity. Regardless of the situation, he would always affirm, "Whatever happens, happens for the good."

During a royal tour with his ministers, the king found himself ambushed by enemies along the way. With valor and the support of his loyal ministers, the king courageously fought back. However, in the midst of this skirmish, the king lost one of his fingers. In great pain, the minister tried to uplift the king's spirits, assuring him, "Do not despair, Your Majesty. Remember, whatever happens, happens for the good." Unexpectedly, the king, overwhelmed by pain and anger, ordered his soldiers to arrest the minister, sentencing him to imprisonment.

Days turned into nights as the king ventured into the dense forest for a hunting expedition. Soon, he found himself lost, chasing after a prey. Fate had a different plan in store for him, for he stumbled upon a fearsome tribe of barbarians. In accordance with their customs, the tribesmen swiftly captured and imprisoned the king, preparing for his sacrificial ritual. The king knew that his survival seemed improbable.

As the preparations for his sacrifice reached their climax, the tribesmen noticed the king's severed finger. In their beliefs, it was deemed inauspicious to sacrifice a disfigured individual. Without hesitation, they released the king, sparing his life. Back in his palace, the king realized that his severed finger had played a vital role in saving him. The minister's words echoed in his mind—"whatever happens, happens for the good." Filled with remorse, the king immediately ordered the release of the minister.

As the minister stood before the king, he humbly accepted the apology and listened intently to the king's tale of escape. Finally, the king inquired, "While it is true that my severed finger brought me salvation, how could it be good for you to endure imprisonment?" With a serene smile, the minister replied, "Your Highness, had I not been in jail, you would have insisted on accompanying you. Thus, I would have suffered the same fate as you—imprisoned by the tribesmen. They spared you due to your disfigurement, but my sacrifice would have been inevitable. Imprisonment saved my life, and therefore, everything that unfolded was ultimately for the best."

This story mirrors our own lives. Certain events may initially appear unfavorable, yet they harbor the potential for countless blessings in the future. By adopting a positive perspective, you can uncover these hidden possibilities.

Exploring into the essence of challenges, you encounter a second profound mantra: "Whatever happens, happens for the good." Hold these two mantras—living in the present and believing in the inherent goodness of all that transpires. They serve as gateways to a profound approach in navigating challenges.

Challenges are Opportunities

CHAPTER 3
Positive Mind System

There was a farmer residing in a quaint village, his humble abode filled with a vibrant flock of chickens. One day, an unexpected visitor found its way to his farm—an eagle's offspring, lost and bewildered. The young eagle assimilated into the flock, mimicking the behavior of its newfound companions. As perplexing as it seemed, the farmer found solace in the eagle's presence, believing that its integration would safeguard the chickens from harm.

Days turned into months, and the baby eagle grew amidst the feathery camaraderie of its adopted family. It pecked at grains alongside its avian companions and roamed the ground, mirroring the familiar patterns of the chickens. The farmer, witnessing this transformation, felt a pang of sorrow deep within. He yearned for the eagle to soar through the boundless skies, yet it seemed that its ability to fly had withered away or perhaps lay dormant, waiting to be awakened.

A pivotal moment arrived when a marauding dog threatened the very existence of the chicken flock. In that perilous moment, the eagle possessed the power to drive away the intruder and protect its newfound family. However, it remained oblivious to its true potential, its wings grounded by the limitations of its surroundings. Rather than rising up with courage and strength, it succumbed to the same fear-driven response as the chickens.

Regrettably, the eagle met the same fate as its avian companions, falling prey to the dog's relentless pursuit.

This allegory echoes a profound truth that resonates in the lives of many. Countless individuals possess extraordinary gifts and talents, yet they remain oblivious to their own capabilities, entrapped within the confines of mediocrity. Society's collective influence often compels individuals to conform, suppressing their unique qualities and hindering their true potential. They find themselves running alongside the masses, mirroring the actions of those around them, unaware of the greatness they possess within.

It is crucial to recognize that you, like the eagle, are born with remarkable abilities waiting to be unleashed. Accepting your individuality and knowing your strengths can empower you to transcend the ordinary and reach extraordinary heights. By breaking free from the herd mentality, you have the potential not only to save yourself from a life of unfulfilled dreams but also to uplift and inspire others along your journey.

Challenges and Self-Image

I have told you the captivating tale of the baby eagle, for within its narrative lies a profound lesson. This lesson revolves around a pivotal concept known as self-image—a reflection of your very mindset.

You may already be acquainted with the notion of self-image, but let us dive deeper into its essence. At its core, self-image represents your perception of self—how you view your personality, approach the world, and ultimately define your own identity. In its simplest form, self-image is the mental picture we construct, comprising our physical, emotional, social, spiritual, and cognitive aspects.

The significance of self-image cannot be understated, as a poor self-image begets a cascade of challenges. Those profoundly impacted by it find themselves ensnared in a perpetual cycle of disappointments, while even those less afflicted exhibit vulnerability during times of adversity. When faced with even the smallest of problems, individuals harboring a negative self-image tend to succumb to stress rather than rise above it. Yet surrendering to challenges is akin to signing a pact of self-sabotage, for challenges are transient, while resilience paves the path to growth.

Fear becomes the unwelcome companion of those plagued by a weakened self-image. These individuals tremble at the mere thought of attempting something new, even if inspired to do so. Doubts loom large, overshadowing any glimmer of confidence in their ability to succeed. The fear of failure grips them so tightly that the prospect of victory becomes unfathomable.

Any worthy pursuit demands unwavering mental focus. Individuals burdened by a diminished self-image seldom attain such concentration. Their minds become entangled in a web of countless thoughts, simultaneously assessing the probabilities of triumph and defeat. As a result, their efforts remain diluted, lacking the potency required to achieve desired outcomes.

The repercussions of a weakened self-image are manifold. In truth, it is the bedrock of a feeble mentality—a mentality that recoils in fear at the mere sight of challenges. To transform challenges into opportunities, it becomes imperative to cultivate a robust self-image. Such an image serves as the cornerstone of a system designed to conquer adversity.

Self-Image Discovery

Deep down, you yearn to cultivate a positive mindset and nurture a resilient self-image. Yet, in this vast world, only a select few seem to achieve such a state of being. Have you ever pondered why this is the case? What causes an individual's self-image to waver? Does nature predestine some to be strong while others remain weak? Are most individuals inherently ill-equipped to tackle life's challenges?

It appears not. When you entered this world, your mind possessed unparalleled strength. Fear was but a distant concept, and failure held no sway over your spirit. If you doubt my words, observe the sheer determination of a young child. A child encounters a fallen straw upon the ground, and without hesitation, endeavors to lift it. Despite initial failures, they persist, undeterred by the laughter echoing around them. Unfazed by the absence of assistance, their sole focus remains on grasping that humble straw. Failure after failure, they persevere until finally, triumphant, the straw rests in their tiny hands. This innate ability resides within every child worldwide—a testament to their unwavering resolve.

So why does the unyielding dedication and indomitable willpower of childhood gradually wane over time? The reasons behind this gradual shift are manifold. The circumstances in which a child grows, the manner in which they are taught, the environment that envelops them, and the individuals they encounter—all play a crucial role. Simply put, their minds undergo a process of programming that diverts them from their innate potential.

Reflect upon the tale of the eagle shared earlier in this chapter, and the game of programming becomes lucid. Just as the offspring of an eagle, possessing extraordinary abilities, loses them due to misguided programming, so too does a typical child lose their inherent capabilities through erroneous programming. In essence, this flawed programming begets a weakened self-image—a foundation upon which all subsequent challenges arise.

While a robust self-image paves the path to success, a feeble one repels success at every turn. Your self-image mirrors your essence; it delineates the boundaries of your capabilities, dictating what you can and cannot achieve. A weakened self-image constricts your potential, constructing a comfortable enclosure within which you gradually confine yourself. Over time, these self-imposed boundaries solidify, rendering them seemingly insurmountable.

With a weakened self-image, even the most rudimentary challenges become daunting. Stepping beyond your comfort zone becomes an arduous feat, conversing with new acquaintances fills you with trepidation, venturing into uncharted territory evokes fear, and seizing novel opportunities becomes a distant dream. Suspicion clouds even the slightest glimmer of achievement, hindering the full utilization of your innate abilities.

Strengthening how you see yourself sets you on a transformative path to success. This involves acknowledging your strengths, realizing their full potential, and confidently moving towards your goals. A strong self-image unlocks your abilities and opens doors to endless opportunities.

Transforming Your Self-Image with a Positive Mindset

Can a weak self-image be fortified? Is it possible to rectify any misguided programming that may have occurred? The answer is a resounding yes. Today, right now, you have the opportunity to begin this transformative journey. Let us dive deeper into this concept.

Your mind operates akin to a sophisticated computer system, functioning on a programmed basis. When you lack awareness of this process, control over your own life slips from your grasp. However, once you become conscious of this programming, you inherently begin to regain command over your existence.

Crucially, you must recognize that you did not enter this world pre-programmed. Everything you have learned has been acquired during your time here. Consequently, the solution lies within your reach. Reprogramming, a common practice to eradicate flawed programming, operates through a dual process. On one hand, you weaken negative emotions, while simultaneously strengthening positive emotions.

Complete eradication of negativity is unattainable, as external events and negative individuals may persist in your surroundings. Occasionally, circumstances may spiral out of your control. However, while negativity cannot be entirely banished, it can be weakened to the point of ineffectiveness. Achieving this entails reinforcing positive emotions.

Rather than focusing on individual positive emotions, I shall illuminate the amalgamation of these emotions that plays an instrumental role in your success. This amalgamation is commonly referred to as a positive attitude. Observe any accomplished individual across the globe, and you will find this quality permeating their being. Attitude serves as the linchpin of their triumph.

Sadly, in this world, people frequently discuss "attitude" without truly comprehending its essence. Some even wield attitude as a negative attribute, often conflating it with pride or ego. Rest assured; you must distance yourself from such misconceptions.

In truth, attitude encapsulates an approach that shapes both the state and trajectory of your life. It represents how you steer existence—an extension of your mindset. Your perception, understanding, and reactions to life's intricacies are directly influenced by attitude. Put simply, attitude serves as a reflection of your values and beliefs.

Now, how does a positive attitude take form? To unravel this enigma, focus on a single word: values. Values lie at the core of attitude. From the earliest stages of your life, you absorb various values from your environment. Take a moment to recognize the values present in your surroundings. Through different life experiences, you internalize certain values, progressively shaping your persona.

Religious teachings and scientific perspectives alike emphasize the development of virtues and samskaras, recognizing their profound impact on both the mind and body. The significance of values stems from the beliefs they engender. Different values give rise to distinct beliefs, which, over time, solidify and shape your worldview. Ultimately, these beliefs form the bedrock of your attitude.

To grasp the concept of attitude, envision it as a three-step process. First, certain values form the foundation, from which beliefs are derived. These beliefs then coalesce into attitudes. It is through this lens that your self-image assumes strength or weakness. Attitude delineates the boundaries of your self-worth. The more positive your attitude, the stronger your self-image becomes.

Acquiring a positive attitude offers a straightforward solution. Consider it a dosage of positivity—an antivirus that identifies and eradicates any lurking viruses within your system. Both negativity and positivity possess the power to flourish. If you harbor anger, it propagates, giving rise to detrimental qualities like arrogance, vengeance, jealousy, and remorse. Conversely, love nurtured within your mind blossoms into virtues such as forgiveness, mercy, compassion, and equanimity. Therefore, it is paramount to sow the seeds of positivity in your mind.

Negativity possesses an alarming speed of growth, capable of infiltrating your thoughts swiftly. Therefore, it is crucial to remain vigilant and prevent any seeds of negativity from taking root in your mind. Instead, nurture the plant of positivity, allowing it to flourish and thrive. The direct consequences of cultivating positivity will manifest in your life, permeating every aspect. With a consistently positive attitude, you will find yourself empowered to succeed in all your endeavors.

Begin this transformative journey with unwavering determination. Believe in your ability to reshape your self-image and transcend the limitations that may have hindered you in the past. You possess the innate power to reprogram your mind and unlock your full potential.

Start by consciously weakening negative emotions, refusing to allow them to hold sway over your thoughts. Challenge the validity of negative beliefs and replace them with positive affirmations that bolster your self-esteem and confidence. Surround yourself with uplifting influences and seek out individuals who embody the positive qualities you aspire to cultivate within yourself.

A Positive Approach to Overcoming Challenges

When tough times run into us, lots of people know about hope and goodness but find it hard to use them. The key lies in making a conscious effort to harness a positive mindset. When navigating through challenging times, it may initially appear daunting to put concepts like a strong self-image into practice. However, rest assured that by allowing positivity to permeate your being, its transformative effects will naturally unfold. Just like achieving complete physical fitness, you are starting on a journey to cultivate a resilient mindset—one that enables you to confront challenges head-on and seize opportunities.

To start this transformative process, you only need to make some small mental efforts that lead to big outcomes. To help you, here are five powerful mental tricks that will boost your resilience for any challenge you face:

1. Change Your Attitude towards Challenges

Ordinarily, when asked to adopt a positive outlook, most individuals find no qualms in doing so. However, when facing adversity, the same advice may seem incomprehensible. Life often presents us with back-to-back problems that seem ceaseless and insurmountable. It is during such moments that many people succumb to despair, losing hope and surrendering. But not you. Defeat is not your destiny. You were born a winner—a conqueror of obstacles. It is time to unleash the victorious spirit within.

Begin by adopting the mindset of a winner. Gain a clear understanding of the exact nature of your problem by articulating it in writing. Clarity empowers you to make informed choices in your response. Once you grasp the true essence of the problem, you can categorize it as a decision, a challenge, or a dilemma.

Accurately identifying the nature of the problem is the initial step towards finding new solutions. Remember, problems are best approached when viewed from the perspective of their potential resolutions. Regardless of how adverse external circumstances may appear, refuse to allow defeat to infiltrate your thoughts. Ignorance and fear are the formidable foes of problem-solving, for they reinforce one another. Fear obstructs the acquisition of knowledge capable of dispelling ignorance, while ignorance, in turn, intensifies fear.

Occasionally, you may find yourself so accustomed to the presence of problems in your life that when an opportunity arises to rid yourself of them, you unwittingly resist. This peculiar phenomenon may seem puzzling, yet it holds true. Some individuals continuously grapple with financial issues, despite subconsciously pushing potential solutions away.

In moments of self-reflection, ask yourself an honest question about long standing problems: Do you genuinely desire to overcome them? If the answer is yes, then what concerted efforts are you making each day to alleviate them?

The path to resolution can be simple or complex, depending on the nature of the problem at hand. Simple problems may warrant practical solutions, while complex issues demand a well-crafted plan that propels you beyond the confines of your current predicament. Such a plan equips you with the necessary tools to comprehend the problem thoroughly and enact the necessary changes.

The human mind gravitates towards simplicity. To steer uncertainty and ambiguity, it is imperative to observe your reactions and transform negative responses into positive ones. By redirecting negative reactions, you pave the way for finding the right solutions. As you get on this transformative journey, the landscape of problems will gradually shift, and you will discover that solutions abound.

2. Break Free from Preconceived Notions

One of the primary obstacles that often plague individuals and hinder their progress in life are preconceived notions. It is all too common for people to carry the weight of a problem in their minds even before the problem materializes. This stems from flawed programming and serves as the genesis of many challenges.

Oftentimes, individuals find themselves pre-judging the outcome of a meeting before it even takes place. They ponder whether the encounter will be beneficial or detrimental, inadvertently closing themselves off to potentially rewarding opportunities. Moreover, prejudices lead people to harbor numerous expectations, only to face disappointment when those expectations go unmet. Occasionally, individuals may even perceive such unmet expectations as an affront to their self-worth, and may stubbornly persist in asserting their viewpoint, thereby giving birth to negative situations.

Prejudice exacts a toll on every aspect of your life. Consider a scenario where you are engaged in business dealings, and you make assumptions about a particular client, deeming them to be of no value to you. Similarly, you harbor expectations about another client, anticipating significant gains. But what happens when these assumptions fail to materialize? You are left feeling regretful or enraged—either way, you suffer a loss.

This phenomenon extends to your personal life as well. There may be instances where you take a friend or partner for granted, presuming they will unconditionally agree with you. Succumbing to these preconceived notions leads to the accumulation of expectations. And when these expectations remain unfulfilled, anger ensues. The repercussions of this dynamic are evident in strained relationships, with unrealistic expectations serving as a significant catalyst for marital discord.

People often begin regarding their expectations as needs—for instance, demanding absolute compliance from a spouse in even the most trivial matters or insisting that children fulfill certain expectations regardless of the circumstances. This endless cycle persists throughout life, unwittingly perpetuating self-inflicted turmoil caused by preconceived notions. Sadly, this thinking becomes ingrained as a habit, without the individual even realizing it.

However, breaking free from the shackles of preconception is not an insurmountable task. The root cause of this predicament lies in erroneous programming. You become a product of your environment. Expectations flourish in the world around you, and you grow up conforming to these expectations. Some notions have already taken root within your mind. Rejecting someone based on their appearance, social class, physical imperfections, or any other superficial reason—what purpose does this serve? While you may have been taught certain things and absorbed certain beliefs, is this assumption truly beneficial in any way?

To liberate yourself from this cycle, there are three essential steps you must undertake. Firstly, understand that you too can be fallible. Admitting a mistake does not diminish your worth; it is a sign of humility. Every human being is prone to making errors, and it is better to acknowledge them rather than attempting to conceal them.

Secondly, nurture your understanding. Allow positive influences to permeate your mind. Just as the adage goes, "garbage in, garbage out," if you fill your mind with negativity, that is all you will emit. Instead, consciously expose yourself to positive ideas and perspectives. Genuine understanding flourishes when you perceive situations for what they truly are.

Lastly, dismantle the barriers within your mind. Engage in open and honest communication with others. Do not hesitate to seek clarification when you encounter something you do not understand. Similarly, if someone declines your services, there is no harm in seeking feedback to improve yourself and your offerings.

By discarding the habit of prejudice, you will witness the resolution of many problems that once plagued your life.

3. Take off the burden of mistakes.

It is not uncommon to stumble and make mistakes in the journey of life. However, what truly sets individuals apart is how they respond to those mistakes. Viewing mistakes as burdens rather than opportunities for growth is where the real problem lies.

As you steer through various aspects of life, be it in the business arena or your personal relationships, it is only natural to encounter missteps along the way. You may inadvertently miss a valuable opportunity, lose a customer, cause some unintended damage, or find yourself entangled in unforeseen circumstances. Perhaps you had a falling out with someone, failed to meet an obligation, or struggled to meet a deadline. These are instances that, knowingly or unknowingly, become a part of your journey. So, what should you do in such situations?

Regardless of the magnitude of the mistake, adopting the same mindset is crucial. The best way to approach mistakes is by acknowledging them. Unfortunately, many individuals shy away from accepting their mistakes. They resort to falsehoods or attempt to cover them up, sometimes even resorting to blame-shifting. However, by succumbing to these tendencies, a person harbors negative emotions within themselves, which permeate all areas of their life. Their reputation suffers, and they begin to spiral downwards. It is essential, therefore, to learn how to address mistakes effectively.

As I've mentioned before, one mistake often leads to another. Thus, it is vital to cultivate the ability to accept your mistakes. If your actions have impacted others, try to understand their perspective. Put yourself in their shoes and develop empathy within yourself. Take responsibility for your actions rather than engaging in a blame game. Assess the circumstances surrounding the mistake and contemplate how you can rectify the situation. Accepting your mistakes does not mean merely playing the role of a guilty party, awaiting punishment. Taking responsibility entails actively seeking solutions to problems.

Admitting one's mistakes is not an easy task; it requires courage. However, if you dare to confront your mistakes, your life will undoubtedly improve. Many individuals carry the burdens of their mistakes throughout their lives, remaining buried under the weight of past errors. Therefore, it is crucial to steer your thoughts in a constructive direction. If necessary, offer sincere apologies and take steps towards resolution. It is important to remember that admitting your mistakes may not always lead to an immediate solution. External circumstances are beyond your control. Nevertheless, even in such situations, do what is right. Some wounds heal with time, so patience may be necessary.

Transform your mistakes into opportunities for learning and growth. There is a saying that goes, "If you have made fewer mistakes in life, it means you haven't ventured far." This sentiment holds true. The greatest individuals in history have made countless mistakes early on in their lives. Accomplished entrepreneurs have faced failures in their businesses. However, what sets them apart is their ability to adopt those mistakes, learn from them, and forge ahead.

Having the right attitude towards mistakes can elevate you into a great leader. When you take ownership of your mistakes and demonstrate responsibility, it paves the way for learning and growth. By setting an example, you inspire others to follow suit. This principle applies to your personal relationships as well. If individuals were more open and courageous in admitting their mistakes, many unnecessary problems would cease to exist.

Mistakes are an inevitable part of life. To minimize their occurrence, you must reduce the likelihood of making them. Rather than running away from mistakes or lamenting over them, the most effective solution lies in embracing them, learning from them, and forging ahead.

4. Develop a Resilient Mental Armor to Overcome Challenges.

The key to success lies in forging ahead, undeterred by the obstacles that come your way. However, many people find themselves easily affected by even the slightest difficulties. Their pace slows down, and sometimes they even come to a complete halt. It becomes a habit to compromise with circumstances and allow themselves to be swayed by every little thing. To counteract this, it is crucial for you to construct a robust mental shield.

People often seek to impress those who offer little resistance, individuals who are unable to challenge negative thoughts and perceive situations objectively. When someone utters a few negative words, they readily accept them. Even if you try to maintain mental strength, when you encounter repetitive negativity, you may find yourself succumbing to it. Sometimes individuals join forces, presenting their arguments collectively to amplify their impact. At times, emotional appeals are made in an attempt to sway your decisions. However, it is essential to discern what is right for you based on reality. External influences often divert your attention, causing you to repeatedly deviate from your intended path, ultimately preventing you from reaching your true destination.

You can diminish this influence by constructing a mental shield. Craft an image of yourself that signals to others that you are not easily swayed. Resisting temptations is not an effortless task. Occasionally, your mind may be enticed by negative attractions, and people may actively attempt to draw you towards them. However, it is essential to resist these detrimental allurements in order to progress. Through repeatedly rejecting these temptations, you can train your mind to steer clear of them. Moreover, people will think twice before attempting to negatively influence you.

External influence does not solely entail being swayed by external individuals. In fact, you may encounter such situations in your everyday life, where others may question your thoughts, advise you to alter your life's course, or even urge you to sever personal relationships. Emotional connections can weaken your resistance and make it easier for others to impose their perspectives upon you. Hence, you must remain cautious.

Experience plays a significant role in developing your mental armor. Throughout your life, you encounter numerous individuals, each with their own ideologies. Take the time to understand them, learn from their experiences, and familiarize yourself with diverse perspectives. This understanding enables you to grasp why someone might hold a particular belief and how significant it is for you. Does the person genuinely have your best interests at heart? These are the questions you must seek answers to.

Oftentimes, immediate reactions guide your behavior. However, it is beneficial to take a moment and ponder. Engaging in thoughtful reflection is advantageous. If you find yourself caught in a mental conflict, take some time alone. Contemplate ideas, seek understanding, and only then make your decision.

The wisdom you possess is measured by the decisions you make for yourself. True wisdom is achieved when you decide without being swayed by external influences. By constructing a mental shield, you can shield yourself from negativity, repel negative individuals, base your decisions on active thinking, enhance your confidence, and effortlessly attain your goals.

5. Increase emotional understanding.

Emotional understanding begins with a deep awareness of your own feelings. It's crucial to be honest with yourself about your emotions. Many people conceal their true feelings, but it's important to recognize that this approach is not beneficial. If anger arises within you, pretending to express love instead would be disingenuous. It's essential to either prevent anger from arising or, if it does, allow it to be expressed. Remember, overcoming negative emotions is a process that requires time and self-compassion.

Suppressing or harboring emotions is not a healthy practice. Instead, emotions should be acknowledged and expressed. Individuals who freely express themselves tend to experience greater happiness in their lives. Moreover, those who have the courage to reveal their genuine emotions often enjoy a higher level of acceptance.

To truly understand the feelings of others, it is imperative that you first become fully aware of your own emotions. Engage in a simple yet effective practical exercise: twice a day, take a moment to ask yourself how you are feeling. This introspective act unveils a spectrum of emotions within you, much like waves rising and falling. Harness this opportunity to sit with your emotions, especially the negative ones. Avoid hastily dismissing them and refrain from passing judgment based solely on immediate feelings. Instead, contemplate when was the last time you experienced a particular negative emotion.

This reflection enables you to discern whether the emotion is a response to the present moment or a remnant of past experiences. Proceed to assess each feeling individually and examine their connection to your thoughts. Throughout this process, pay attention to the sensations in your body. Are feelings of fear causing a tightness in your stomach? Has your heart rate increased as you imagined a certain scenario? Heightening your awareness in this manner allows you to unravel your true emotions.

Once your emotional states are clear, it's time to direct them purposefully. Ask yourself: What is stimulating this emotion? Is it leading me towards a constructive conclusion? By addressing these questions, you can realign yourself with a positive mindset. Aim to amplify the positive emotions within you and diminish the negative ones. Managing your emotions is a skill that involves maximizing the potential of positive emotions while minimizing the impact of negative ones.

6. The Power of Mental Problem-Solving.

You hold the key to solving your problems, and it's time to accept this truth. Many people inadvertently exacerbate their problems by assuming that someone else will come to their rescue. They fall into a dangerous illusion, where they rely heavily on others for solutions. By doing so, they relinquish control of their own lives, making it easier to assign blame if their problems persist. This pattern gradually becomes a habit.

Those who seek external solutions often find themselves facing even more problems. They become susceptible to deception, particularly when dealing with serious challenges. It is essential, therefore, to shift the focus inward—to find the solution within yourself. Whether you believe it or not, the answer to every problem lies within you, before it can be found externally.

Discovering internal solutions empowers you to cultivate self-reliance. First and foremost, recognize that you possess the capacity to find a solution. Far too often, people attribute their struggles to luck or external factors. They blame the examiner for receiving lower marks in an exam or the judges for losing a competition. At every stage of life, they find someone else to hold responsible. While there may be some truth to these circumstances, it is vital that you prioritize what you can do on your own. If you feel that your talent is being overlooked, strive to elevate it to such heights that it cannot be ignored. Dedicate yourself to continuous self-improvement until you become an irresistible force. Regardless of the area of life you find yourself in, set your sights on reaching the pinnacle of success.

Engage in the following mental exercise: Find a comfortable space and quiet your mind. Reflect on what you can personally do to address the problem at hand. Devise a strategy within your thoughts and articulate it clearly. Examine each point meticulously before starting on the path towards a solution. Through this exercise, you will uncover solutions to many challenging problems.

Life is full of inevitable obstacles, but fretting about them will get you nowhere. When you actively seek solutions, you liberate yourself from worry. Adopt the belief that you will find a solution, no matter the circumstances. By internalizing and implementing the concepts you have dived into thus far, your life will become remarkably easier. You will forge ahead undeterred by external circumstances, armed with the ability to tackle any challenge that comes your way.

Next Step: Read this book: "Subconscious Mind: Master Your Subconscious and Achieve Happiness & Success." With this book achieve lasting happiness and discover actionable steps to rewire your thoughts, paving the way for genuine happiness in every facet of life. You can find this book through my author profile or just visit: selfhelppowers.com/books/

CHAPTER 4
Your Winning Strategy

There is a smaller country in the world – Singapore. Yet, there is hardly any nation that can overlook Singapore's influence on the global stage. This city-state has emerged as a vital hub for trade and finance, making it an essential player in international affairs. While there are numerous factors contributing to this prominence, it is Singapore's exceptional governance and strategic economic policies that truly set it apart.

Geographically located at the crossroads of major shipping routes, Singapore is surrounded by larger neighbors, yet it has carved out a reputation as one of the most competitive economies in the world. Despite its limited land and natural resources, Singapore has transformed itself into a thriving metropolis, attracting multinational corporations and businesses from around the globe. The nation's remarkable journey to success began after gaining independence in 1965, a time when it faced significant challenges, including high unemployment and social unrest. However, through strategic planning and a focus on education and infrastructure, Singapore turned adversity into opportunity.

At the core of Singapore's success lies its commitment to effective governance and a pro-business environment. The government has prioritized transparency, efficiency, and anti-corruption measures, creating a stable and attractive landscape for investors. Moreover, the nation's education system emphasizes not only academic excellence but also critical thinking and innovation, producing a skilled workforce ready to meet the demands of a rapidly changing global economy.

One significant aspect of Singapore's strategy is its emphasis on multiculturalism and social cohesion. By promoting inclusivity among its diverse population, Singapore fosters a sense of unity and shared purpose, which is essential for national stability and progress. Additionally, the nation has invested heavily in sustainable development, aiming for a green economy that balances growth with environmental responsibility.

The success of Singapore's economic model has drawn the attention of countries worldwide, eager to learn from its achievements. Many nations have sent delegations to study Singapore's policies and practices, recognizing its dedication to continual improvement and innovation as a blueprint for prosperity.

Observing Singapore's accomplishments, it becomes clear that regardless of the size of a nation or the challenges it faces, determination and strategic planning can lead to remarkable success. Singapore's ability to steer obstacles and leverage its unique strengths is a powerful reminder that with foresight and resilience, we too can overcome challenges and thrive in an interconnected world.

Need of an Upgraded Strategy

As you observe Singapore's remarkable transformation into a global economic powerhouse, you may wonder why larger nations have not overshadowed its influence despite its small size. The truth is, Singapore's progress has not been without challenges. However, its unwavering determination and steadfast policies have created an environment where potential competitors think twice before underestimating its capabilities. Consider this: a nation that can thrive in a region filled with larger economies and emerge as a leader in trade and finance compels deep reflection.

The essence of Singapore's success lies in its steadfast belief in the power of innovative governance and strategic adaptability. Its economic model is in a constant state of evolution, continuously responding to global trends and challenges. In times of adversity, you too require such a forward-thinking approach.

Now, reflect upon your own journey. You have progressed, leaving behind the burdens of "what if," "why not," and "what's next." You have understood the significance of a positive mindset and a robust self-image as tools for conquering these concerns. You comprehend the importance of living in the present moment, accepting it for what it is. It is time to formulate an action plan, for you have acquired sufficient understanding of how to confront challenges and transform them into opportunities.

While your challenges may appear daunting, rest assured that you possess the capability to overcome each one. Just as Singapore has turned its limitations into advantages, believe that, with determination, you can transform challenges into opportunities in every aspect of your life. This chapter serves as your guide to an action plan specifically designed for this purpose. If you have absorbed the wisdom presented thus far, the path ahead will be remarkably smooth, paving the way for your own success story.

The Magic of Goal Setting Still Holds True!

If you are already familiar with the concept of goal setting, that is wonderful. If you have been propelling yourself forward by setting and pursuing goals, even better. This familiarity will facilitate your comprehension of certain concepts. However, if you are unfamiliar with the transformative power of goal setting, fret not. It will not be difficult for you to grasp its essence.

Often, during normal circumstances, individuals progress by aligning themselves with goals, dreams, and the pursuit of success. However, when challenges multiply, attention tends to veer away from these aspirations. And when I refer to goals, I am not solely referring to business objectives but also the goals of your personal life.

Difficult situations and challenges have a tendency to dismantle our well-laid plans. Sometimes, the enormity of the challenge causes individuals to abandon their dreams and goals, focusing solely on surviving the crisis at hand. Yet, this should not be the case. If you aspire to transform your challenges into opportunities, you need the guiding force of strong goals. Without a well-defined plan of action, without a robust strategy in place, it becomes exceedingly difficult to make progress.

Undoubtedly, the magic of goal setting remains potent even in the face of the most formidable challenges. All you need to do is fine-tune your strategy, and its influence will manifest. Let us dive deeper into the intricacies of this transformative process.

Basic Principles of Goal Setting

To truly comprehend the magic of goal setting, it is essential to grasp its fundamental principles. Let us explore some key points without delving too deeply into the intricacies.

Goals empower you to pursue your aspirations. They propel you towards your desired destinations and enable you to achieve the balance you seek in life. By setting and striving for goals, you shape your character and become the person you aspire to be.

Goals represent the deepest desires within you, igniting your motivation to continually grow. They serve as bridges between your dreams and reality, propelling you forward on your journey. When you set goals, you hold yourself accountable for your actions, transcending mere contemplation and actively engaging in the necessary tasks. The beauty of this practice lies in its ability to enhance your efficiency and effectiveness over time.

To set the right goals, you must have a clear understanding of who you are, what you are doing, and where you are headed. These self-awareness questions form the foundation upon which well-aligned goals are built. Goals come with a guarantee of facilitating the accomplishment of any task effortlessly.

Goal setting adheres to certain principles that are vital to comprehend. One of the most critical aspects is writing down your goals. You may have heard of the magic inherent in written goals. When goals remain confined to thoughts alone, they lack the transformative power that written goals possess. However, once committed to paper, goals manifest into reality. This technique has been adopted by the world's most successful individuals, and psychologists support its efficacy, backed by scientific evidence. The act of writing down your dreams and goals taps into a deeper world of consciousness, thoughts, and productivity—the wellspring of your subconscious mind. It is a powerful exercise in harnessing your mental faculties.

Writing goals also entails employing a particular technique. Always express your goals in the present tense. Avoid the common practice of writing them in the future tense, as it detracts from your sense of immediacy and awareness. Write your goals by hand on paper, allowing your thoughts to flow from pen to page. While some individuals opt for digital means of recording goals, leveraging modern technology, there is a special connection and impact that comes from writing them with your own hand. Clearly articulate your goals, ensuring they are legible and comfortably written. Take your time; do not rush through the process of documenting your goals.

As you commit your goals to paper, it is crucial to visualize them. Allow your mind to vividly imagine the attainment of these goals. Before writing, release any self-imposed limitations. Disregard constraints related to your current circumstances, available resources, time, or finances. Enter the world of goal setting with a limitless mindset.

Each goal should be clearly articulated. Define the level of achievement you desire in your business endeavors, the financial abundance you seek, the happiness you aspire to in your personal life, the fitness milestones you aim to reach, your desire to contribute to society, the reputation you envision for yourself, and the spiritual experiences you long for.

It's natural for some goals to be long-term or monumental in nature, requiring a significant amount of time to achieve. Whatever the case may be, it's crucial to establish a realistic deadline for yourself. Determine the timeframe within which you aim to accomplish your goal. If others have achieved similar goals in a shorter time span, you can use their achievements as a benchmark for setting your own target. Remember, no goal is unrealistic, but deadlines can be. Therefore, exercising careful consideration when setting deadlines is essential.

Assess your available time and resources, gaining clarity on how much time you can realistically dedicate to the pursuit of your goal. Oftentimes, individuals mistakenly assume they can achieve a goal in the shortest possible time, only to be left disappointed when their desired outcome is not attained. Conversely, some people allocate an excessive amount of time to their goals, resulting in a lack of motivation and ultimately abandoning their aspirations.

Striving for a balanced and realistic deadline is paramount. Deadlines serve as a powerful tool, heightening your consciousness of your goals. Think of them as mental alarms that keep you on track. Once you've ingrained a deadline in your mind, you naturally become more committed to meeting that deadline. Remember, some goals may span years—two, five, or even ten—while others are more modest, with a timeframe of weeks or months.

Once you've established a deadline, effective implementation is key. Here's where a special technique comes into play: breaking down your goals into smaller, manageable parts. These smaller goals are inherently more attainable, acting as stepping stones towards accomplishing your larger objective. So, take your big goals and break them down into smaller, bite-sized targets.

Let's illustrate this concept with a simple example. Imagine you have a 200-page book to read, and you've set a five-day deadline to complete it. First, evaluate your available time. Perhaps you have about two hours each day when you're not engaged in particularly productive activities—time spent commuting, watching television, or using your mobile phone. Over five days, this accumulates to a total of ten hours. By dividing the 200-page book into smaller portions, you realize that reading 20 pages per day is a manageable feat. In other words, by dedicating just one hour to reading, you can cover ten pages, allowing you to effortlessly finish the entire book within the set time frame without disrupting your daily routine. This serves as a straightforward example, but the principle remains the same.

By applying this approach to goal setting, you can achieve any ambition—whether it pertains to your financial pursuits or personal aspirations.

Revamp Your Goals: Redefining and Refocusing

By now, you've grasped the fundamental principles of goal setting, and the magic of this practice has undoubtedly become evident. However, during challenging times, it's easy to lose sight of this magic, succumbing to a negative mindset that hinders us from utilizing its full potential. But fear not! If you approach your challenges with a positive mindset, you can transform them into remarkable opportunities.

Take a moment to assess your current situation and available options. If you find yourself stuck with old goals that have been derailed by challenges, fret not. This is your chance to redefine and refocus your goals. Whether you've been moving forward aimlessly without defined goals or have previously set objectives that have lost momentum, it's time for a fresh start. Define a clear goal for yourself, set a deadline, and forge ahead. During challenging times, redefining old goals and creating new ones is the key to progress.

Now that your goals have been redefined, it's crucial to ensure their implementation. To do this, you must determine your action steps. Here's a simple exercise to help you on this journey. Take a piece of paper, use your computer, or open a digital app to create three columns. In the first column, write down all your goals. Alongside each goal, note any general requirements necessary for their attainment. These could include learning new skills, improving existing ones, networking with new individuals, or securing additional investments. Essentially, identify all the necessary elements for each goal.

Once you've defined your goals, move to the second column and specify a time frame for each objective. Be specific, jotting down actual dates instead of vague timeframes like "a week" or "a couple of days." The third column is the most crucial—it's where you outline your action steps. The number of action steps may vary for each goal, but their purpose is singular: to propel you toward success. Take the time to craft a step-by-step action plan.

Each goal holds a unique level of priority for you. Some objectives will take precedence over others. Correspondingly, identify the action steps in order of priority. Determine which tasks you'll tackle first. With your comprehensive goal list and corresponding action steps in hand, arrange them according to priority. In essence, you now possess a complete blueprint for goal achievement. The time has come to structure your daily routine around this plan.

Just as you plan for the year, month, and week ahead, it's essential to plan for the next day in advance. Decide what you will accomplish the following day. Write down which goal you'll be working on, along with the specific action step to be taken. Daily goals serve as your active targets, keeping you engaged in the journey. They provide an opportunity to work on smaller milestones while keeping your sights set on the bigger picture. Even the smallest tasks become effortless when approached with intention, ultimately leading to significant accomplishments.

Create a separate list for each day and keep it with you. Prioritize your tasks and work through them accordingly. Stick to your predetermined schedule, and you'll witness your progress unfold. Adjust your routine based on the time available to you each day, ensuring that you consistently make strides toward your goals.

The Key to Real Results: Taking Action

Now that you've dived into the depths of goal setting, another crucial aspect comes into focus: implementation. It is through action that you manifest tangible results. When you proclaim your dedication to a goal, you're essentially committing to its implementation. It's evident that without taking action, you cannot expect to see the desired outcomes materialize.

During the implementation phase, there are key considerations that can significantly ease your journey. Firstly, focus on one goal at a time. It's common for people to entertain thoughts of other goals while working on a single task or believe they can tackle multiple objectives simultaneously. However, this approach is flawed.

Your daily goal consists of a few critical tasks that warrant your undivided attention. Allocate more time and energy to these tasks. Disregard all distractions and concentrate solely on completing one task before moving on to the next. It's better to accomplish a few things exceptionally well than to juggle numerous tasks with diminished effectiveness.

You've set your goals, allocated time accordingly, and exerted effort. Yet, it's important to assess the effectiveness of your efforts. Sometimes you persist in your efforts, assuming that the results will be favorable. However, it is essential to pause and evaluate your progress.

Assessment holds numerous benefits. It provides a realistic picture of your current situation. If your efforts aren't yielding the desired outcomes, it's necessary to make adjustments. This allows you to take the necessary steps for improvement. If a task hasn't been executed well, it can be redone with renewed vigor.

Remember, success lies in taking small steps correctly. Dedicate yourself to executing even the smallest tasks with excellence. By accomplishing each small step effectively, you pave the way for the successful completion of the overarching goal.

While the goal itself may remain unchanged, the implementation may require adaptations. Understand that no process is flawless. The possibility of discovering a more efficient approach is ever-present. Any method that enhances your current process, conserves energy and time, is deemed superior. Accept the notion that success is a journey, and goals are the very essence that make this expedition worthwhile. By comprehending the principles of goal setting, you unlock the potential to achieve a perfect balance.

The Optimal Utilization of Available Time

I want to emphasize that time is undoubtedly your most valuable asset. Your ability to utilize it effectively plays a pivotal role in achieving long-lasting success. While lamenting over the time that has already elapsed serves no purpose, it is crucial to make the best use of the time that is presently at your disposal. To accomplish this, it is imperative to devise a well-thought-out strategy for the present day.

Time, in its essence, possesses inherent merits that warrant closer examination. Understanding the nature of time is crucial as I am about to reveal a secret related to time that has the potential to transform your life and resolve your problems. Therefore, let us dive into some fundamental aspects pertaining to time.

Time exists in equal measure for everyone, yet it is inherently limited. However, it is worth noting that individuals have managed to achieve unlimited success and experience various forms of happiness within the confines of this finite resource. If you aspire to reach new heights of success in your own life, it is essential for you to acquaint yourself with the art of time management. You must acknowledge that if others have achieved so much within the same allotted time, then so can you.

Indeed, time management is a remarkable technique that holds the power to exponentially increase your productivity and enable you to attain the success you desire while optimally utilizing your energy. If you so desire, you can attain the happiness you seek.

The successes and failures you encounter throughout your life are contingent upon your ability to make decisions. The more adept you become at making the right decisions in a timely manner, the swifter your journey toward success will be. Effective time management can alleviate the pressure of decision-making and nurture the development of sound judgment. When decisions are made from a place of competence, they tend to be correct, leading to an increase in your significance and enhancing both your personal and professional stature.

The scarcity of time often perpetuated a state of constant stress among individuals. Particularly during challenging times, people often feel that their precious time is being squandered or that they simply lack the time necessary to fulfill their responsibilities.

The art of time management has the remarkable ability to make you feel as though you possess an abundance of time. This perception instills a sense of calm and control within you. As a result, you gain a clearer perspective on the available options and can assess possibilities more effectively. Surprisingly, the art of time management can significantly reduce your stress levels. You begin to believe in your capacity to accomplish anything, which fosters tremendous self-confidence. As you witness the tangible effects of effective time management, your faith in its efficacy grows stronger, and your mind's faculties are fully harnessed.

Allocating free time for oneself is crucial. Every individual requires moments of rest and tranquility. Unfortunately, during challenging periods, finding such moments can prove to be quite difficult. Many individuals struggle to sit quietly for even ten minutes. Nevertheless, your free time can be likened to a substantial deposit in a bank, providing a sense of calm by alleviating unnecessary worries.

Effective time management leaves no room for procrastination. The more diligently you practice it, the more self-discipline you cultivate. This invaluable skill spills over into other areas of your life. Tasks that have eluded completion due to a lack of discipline can now be accomplished as a result of your newfound understanding of time management.

By utilizing your time wisely, you gain the ability to establish and fulfill your priorities effectively. When you determine your priorities, your efforts, behavior, and lifestyle naturally align themselves accordingly. Fixing priorities simplifies the process of exerting effort, and these efforts yield accurate and desired outcomes. Experts concur that the art of prioritization is a skill that must be acquired. Understanding this skill is vital to steer within the confines of time constraints. By doing so, you will successfully achieve all the goals, both personal and professional, that you have set for yourself.

In the upcoming chapters, I will separately discuss professional life and personal life. So far, you have gained valuable insights about the challenges. Now is the opportune moment to put this knowledge into practical use. By examining business life and personal life separately, I will dive into intricate techniques that enable you to transform challenges into opportunities. Following these next two chapters, you will possess a wealth of knowledge that can make a profound difference in your life.

CHAPTER 5
Success In Professional Life

Within the expansive canvas of the Mahabharata, there exists a particular story that profoundly connects with the essence of human nature, providing significant insights for our existence. Today, I would like to share this story, for within its ancient folds lies a timeless truth that can ignite the fire within you.

Hastinapur, the epicenter of conflict between the noble Pandavas and the arrogant Kauravas, witnessed the clash of dreams and aspirations. As the eldest of the brothers, Yudhishthira was destined to ascend the throne, yet Duryodhana vehemently contested his rightful claim. The animosity grew until it reached a boiling point, with Duryodhana even plotting the demise of the Pandavas. Miraculously, the Pandavas escaped unscathed, buoyed by the firm support of the people.

Inevitably, the time came when Yudhishthira's ascendancy to the throne seemed imminent. However, Dhritarashtra, swayed by the tempest of his son's anger, sought a compromise. The kingdom was divided, with the ancestral land of Hastinapur forming the old domain and Khandavprastha, a forsaken forest teeming with venomous serpents, becoming the new abode of the Pandavas. The sight that greeted the Pandavas in Khandavprastha left them astonished.

The dense forest of Khandavprastha seemed an insurmountable obstacle—a mere shadow of the kingdom they had envisioned. Disheartenment threatened to consume them, but amidst the darkness, Krishna, the embodiment of wisdom, stood steadfast. He implored the Pandavas to perceive their challenges as opportunities, urging them to rebuild their desired kingdom from scratch. His words resonated deep within their hearts, for they held the key to transforming adversity into triumph. Though the path ahead appeared daunting, Krishna advised them to take it step by step.

First and foremost, they needed land to construct their new world. To achieve this, the forest had to be vanquished and the venomous serpents subdued. Taking the reins of the chariot, Krishna led the way, while the skilled archer Arjuna unleashed a torrent of fiery arrows upon their serpentine adversaries. Racing ahead, Krishna and Arjuna displayed unwavering determination, their physical prowess matching the strength of their resolve. With each arrow that pierced the air, the forest trembled under the might of their combined effort. Eventually, their indomitable spirit triumphed, reducing the forest and its venomous inhabitants to ash.

Days turned into nights, and with unwavering dedication, the Pandavas finally stood upon a fertile land. Their toil was not in vain. With Krishna's aid and the wealth they had obtained through the partition, they summoned the finest craftsmen of the era. Collaborating with Krishna, they meticulously charted their vision, giving birth to a magnificent city—Indraprastha. Its resplendence captivated the hearts of traders and affluent citizens from Hastinapur, who soon flocked to make Indraprastha their new home. Within a few years, Indraprastha blossomed into a powerful center of influence, radiating prosperity across the world.

This extraordinary tale from the annals of the Mahabharata offers a profound message—one that often eludes us when we merely observe stories unfold. The saga of Indraprastha's creation imparts a crucial wisdom: within the greatest challenges lie the grandest opportunities. The crucial ingredient lies within your grasp; it is the act of seizing those opportunities that sets your journey in motion.

Assess The Challenges of Professional Life

Assessing the challenges that permeate your professional journey is the first step towards unlocking boundless opportunities. By accurately evaluating these obstacles and devising effective solutions, you pave the way for growth and success. Each individual's challenges may vary depending on their unique circumstances, and correspondingly, the opportunities that lie within them are equally diverse. Allow me to shed light on this through illustrative examples.

If you find yourself employed in an industry affected by an economic downturn, consider it a substantial challenge. The looming possibility of salary cuts or job loss can be disconcerting. However, amidst this adversity, lies a silver lining—the opportunity to rise above. It is essential to focus on two pivotal aspects. Firstly, invest in your personal and professional growth by enhancing your professional acumen. Adopt continuous learning and acquire new skills that will be in high demand in the future. Remarkably, acquiring knowledge need not be an exorbitant endeavor; in the information age, a thirst for learning is all you need, as the resources to support your growth are abundantly available.

Secondly, identify niche areas where your unique talents can be leveraged to the fullest. Exceptional individuals are always in demand, and during times of recession, their value becomes even more pronounced. Keep your senses attuned and be proactive in seeking out opportunities that align with your skills. By doing so, you position yourself as a valuable asset, ready to make a meaningful impact.

For those involved in business ventures, a similar dual approach is imperative. On one hand, focus on minimizing unnecessary expenditures, while on the other, maximize your attention on activities that generate the greatest benefits during this period. When confronted with challenges, always respond by understanding the needs of your target audience. People often gravitate towards essential products and services, and it is crucial to tailor your offerings accordingly. Customize your products and services to address their specific requirements. Moreover, ensure that your endeavors are visible and apparent to the public.

Expertise commands admiration and trust. Regardless of whether you are an employee, a self-employed professional, or a business owner, positioning yourself as an expert is of paramount importance. People naturally inclined towards experts, seeking their advice and making use of their expertise. Therefore, it is crucial to establish yourself as an authority in your field. To achieve this, adopt effective strategies that resonate with your audience.

Begin by immersing yourself in your industry and its related subjects. Deepen your knowledge and comprehend the practical applications of each facet. Put these insights into practice, enhancing your understanding through personal experience. Showcase your abilities, harness your creativity, and strive to present yourself in the best possible light. Cultivate your personal brand alongside your business brand. Engage in meaningful conversations on significant issues, amplifying your visibility. By becoming a prominent figure, renowned for your outspoken voice and reputable expertise, you will undoubtedly reap the rewards.

Increase Your Financial Understanding

Elevating your financial understanding holds the key to conquering the challenges that intertwine with monetary matters. In truth, the fabric of human existence is intricately woven with the threads of money. Serving as the conduit for fulfilling our needs, money assumes a dual nature—it can be a source of fulfillment and, at times, a cause for distress. Given its undeniable significance, your lives often revolve around the pursuit of financial stability, inadvertently obscuring the path to true happiness. Therefore, it comes as no surprise that encountering a financial challenge can be the most daunting obstacle of all.

To steer economic challenges with confidence, acquiring a solid foundation of financial knowledge is imperative. This knowledge not only empowers you to earn money ethically but also provides you with the wisdom to invest it judiciously, maximizing your returns.

Unfortunately, traditional education systems have historically neglected the importance of financial literacy. Many people initiate their careers or launch businesses without a full understanding of the complexities associated with finances. Consequently, they find themselves unable to generate sufficient income due to a lack of economic know-how. Those who possess rudimentary knowledge of conventional savings methods often attempt to secure their future through these means. Yet, their illusion of safety swiftly crumbles when confronted with adversity. It is said that a mere six months of unemployment can push an individual into the depths of destitution.

What is Your Real Financial Status?

To succeed in the field of finance, it's vital to assess your present financial situation. The first step toward this journey is understanding the source of your income and determining whether it aligns with your aspirations.

The most prevalent avenue of income for individuals across the globe is employment. Holding a job offers a sense of security unlike other methods. It allows individuals to work for others and receive a steady income to fulfill their basic needs, enabling them to thrive within society.

The advantages of a job lie in its potential to provide stability and a consistent salary, granting a semblance of financial security. You are expected to fulfill your job responsibilities, accept the compensation offered, and proceed with your life. However, it is crucial to recognize that relying solely on a job cannot grant you financial independence.

The primary drawback of employment lies in its time dependency. Ideally, your compensation is commensurate with the hours you invest in your work. Yet, your control remains in the hands of someone else. In times of emergency, you risk losing your job, and a few months of unemployment can swiftly dismantle your financial stability. This realization often propels individuals toward the allure of self-employment, where they can reclaim control over their own destiny.

Self-employment encompasses consultants and individuals who manage their own businesses, assuming sole responsibility for their income. These individuals bear the weight of steering their own lives and circumstances by leveraging their skills, labor, and resources. The advantage lies in the autonomy it offers—an individual can operate according to their desires, free from the reliance on others. However, the significant drawback of self-employment lies in its heavy reliance on the individual and their capabilities. A sudden health problem or an economic catastrophe can swiftly erode everything they have built. Hence, it becomes crucial to expand a small business into a larger enterprise, mitigating risk and utilizing the expertise of others.

A thriving business represents the pinnacle of income generation, harnessed by entrepreneurs and the world's wealthiest individuals. In this context, an individual effectively utilizes the time and efforts of others, multiplying their earnings. The advantage of a successful enterprise lies in the assurance of financial stability as the business flourishes and expands. However, it is vital to acknowledge the challenges associated with managing a large-scale business. A single misstep can lead to substantial losses, and operating a sizable enterprise incurs significant expenses. At times, entrepreneurs may need to rely on investors and financial institutions for support, exposing them to potential upheavals during economic emergencies.

Indeed, business surpasses employment and self-employment in terms of financial potential. However, it is crucial to consider different business models, some requiring substantial capital while others necessitating a larger workforce. Before exploring the intricacies of any business endeavor, focus on the potential profitability it offers. While the size of the business may vary, your ultimate goal should be substantial earnings.

You have the opportunity to earn income through various means, each with its own set of advantages and disadvantages. No choice can guarantee absolute immunity from financial challenges; however, some options may provide greater protection than others. Through comprehending your existing financial situation and thoughtfully choosing a direction that aligns with your aspirations, you can initiate a voyage towards financial empowerment. Remember, the choice lies in your hands, and with perseverance and strategic decision-making, you can steer the challenges that lie ahead.

The Significance of Financial Knowledge in Your Life

Understanding the various avenues of income is a rare trait among individuals in our world today, largely due to the neglect of this topic in traditional education systems. Therefore, it becomes imperative for you to equip yourself with the right economic knowledge before settling on any particular solution. With a sound understanding of finance, you can establish an income system that not only allows you to steer economic challenges with ease but also empowers you to bounce back resiliently from any setbacks. However, it's important to note that familiarizing yourself with different sources of income is merely the first step in acquiring financial knowledge.

Contrary to popular belief, financial knowledge is not solely focused on the accumulation of wealth. There are numerous individuals who earn substantial annual incomes but find themselves discontented with their lives. Despite their financial resources, they continue to grapple with the anxiety surrounding money. This stems from the distinction between scarcity and abundance. Regardless of the amount of money one amasses, uncertainty persists if a mindset of abundance is not cultivated.

Temporarily transitioning from one job to another may seem like a quick fix for your predicament. Similarly, pursuing high-risk investments with the hope of earning quick returns can be no more than a fleeting dream. Relying solely on self-employment places an excessive burden on your shoulders, while establishing a larger business presents its own set of challenges. In such circumstances, it becomes crucial to make informed choices from the available options.

Financial security is a universal aspiration, playing a pivotal role in one's mental well-being. Recognizing this inherent need, insurance and investment companies devise various schemes. Some individuals emphasize investing more, while others prioritize saving diligently. Simultaneously, many people become overly reliant on loans during financial hardships. However, debt merely marks the beginning of a series of adversities in life. Being trapped in the cycle of debt hampers the experience of happiness. Astonishingly, despite this realization, people continue to seek happiness through loans and borrowings. This is where caution is paramount.

Consider the example of individuals who invest their entire capital in purchasing a house, subsequently spending the next three to four decades repaying the loan installments. At the end of their lives, can they truly claim to have attained happiness? Also, the burden of repaying multiple loans leaves little room for joy.

It is challenging to find solutions when you confine your perspective. If your earnings are capped, it is not an obligation to maintain that limit. You possess the power to liberate yourself from this confinement at any time. However, by consistently resorting to loans, you inadvertently reinforce your own imprisonment. This perpetual fear obstructs you from exploring alternative options, rendering compromise a necessity that consumes your entire life. The dire consequences of such a path are evident.

Hence, attaining financial freedom necessitates avoiding debt. Although debt may grant you access to certain material possessions, it cannot deliver true happiness.

In the world of business, loans are a frequent occurrence. However, it is vital for such loans to serve a specific purpose. They should not be acquired as surplus funds to address arbitrary needs; rather, they should be strategic investments that guarantee returns.

Moreover, it is crucial to discern the fundamental disparity between liabilities and assets when considering financial ventures. Investments should enhance your assets, not burden you with liabilities.

Differentiating Between Liabilities and Assets

Within the domain of financial understanding, certain individuals highly prioritize both saving and investing. However, it is crucial to discern whether you are burdening yourself or establishing holdings that will serve as a continuous source of income.

To simplify the concept of burden and holding, we can refer to them as liabilities and assets. This distinction goes beyond mere words; it encompasses a deeper understanding, often leading people to make errors in their application.

In essence, it boils down to increasing assets and reducing liabilities. By grasping this fundamental principle and incorporating it into your economic knowledge, you stand to gain significant benefits.

Regrettably, many individuals tend to amplify their liabilities instead of nurturing their assets, giving rise to various problems. It is essential to gain clarity on this differentiation. Let's dive into it using the previous example of a home loan. Suppose you have acquired a house, which you may consider an asset. However, this may not necessarily be the case, particularly if you have obtained it through a loan. Often, such loans span several years, ranging from 25 to 30 years in some instances. As a result, you become bound by this commitment. Every month, you must shoulder the responsibility of paying the associated bills for the house while also fulfilling the loan installment. Over time, the structure of the house may deteriorate, causing its value to decrease. In this scenario, the house that was once deemed an asset transforms into a liability. Similarly, credit cards, vehicles, or loans can also become liabilities rather than assets.

In essence, the greater the number of liabilities you accumulate, the more susceptible you become to financial challenges. Upon closer inspection, you will notice that wealthy individuals prioritize asset creation, while those who are financially strained or belong to the middle class find themselves entangled in liabilities. True wealth is attained when you possess more assets than liabilities.

An asset contributes to your income, while a liability drains it. To achieve financial prosperity, it is imperative to strike the right balance between your liabilities and assets. Regardless of the amount of money you earn, if your liabilities equal or surpass your assets, you cannot be considered wealthy.

However, reducing your liability does not imply reducing all your expenses. You can still fulfill your needs, but you do so by leveraging your assets. By generating income from your assets, even the most extravagant requirements can be met.

Upon examining the lives of successful individuals, you will discover that those who amass considerable wealth are either involved in asset creation through entrepreneurial endeavors or are satisfying their needs using income generated from their existing assets. Therefore, if your aim is to evade financial challenges in the long run, it is essential to minimize your liabilities and focus on augmenting your assets.

Explore Passive Income Sources

As you begin your financial expedition, it's essential to recognize the significance of passive income. Growing your assets is a long-term endeavor that requires an initial investment. Therefore, it is crucial to include asset-building in your financial goals. If you are determined to overcome your current financial challenges, set new financial goals immediately and take actionable steps towards achieving them. Within these goals, prioritize reducing liabilities and increasing assets. Additionally, there is one vital task that must not be overlooked—establishing alternative income sources.

Relying solely on one source of income can give rise to financial instability. If your livelihood depends solely on a job and you have taken out a loan based on that foundation, any disruption in your employment will undoubtedly impact your situation. Similarly, if a business relies solely on a single product or service, its income will fluctuate with the rise and fall of that particular offering. In such circumstances, it is always beneficial to have an alternative or multiple sources of income. Diversifying your business is equally advantageous.

In essence, it is evident that you need a means of earning money that is not entirely dependent on your active involvement. This is where the concept of passive income comes into play. Passive income refers to money earned consistently with minimal effort or even without any effort at all.

Differentiating between active income and passive income is straightforward. Active income is derived from providing services, such as your regular income from a job or business. However, active income alone cannot make you truly wealthy. It requires your time and effort. On the other hand, passive income can be generated through rental properties, limited partnerships, or other ventures in which you are not actively engaged. The key difference between active income and passive income lies in the element of "effort." Passive income is automatic—it continues to flow even when you are not actively working. Once you establish a passive income stream, it becomes a consistent source of revenue.

Attaining financial freedom hinges on the presence of passive income in your financial portfolio. Generating passive income also necessitates an investment of time, energy, and money. Initially, you invest your time, but the advantage lies in the fact that, over time, there is no need to invest additional time or effort to maintain it.

Time is a finite resource, and your capabilities have limits. That's why it's crucial to adopt methods that enable your money to grow automatically. The more passive your income becomes, the more active your life can be.

Choose the right passive income stream based on your capabilities. Seek options where continuous work is not required. Diversify your sources of income within a reasonable range. While it may take time to establish these sources initially, as you strengthen them, the money will start flowing in effortlessly. By strategically working towards passive income and building your assets, you will achieve financial freedom, allowing you to enjoy a life of abundance.

Unlock Financial Freedom: The Path to Success in Business

Financial freedom is the gateway to breaking free from the constraints of time and money. It holds the key to your happiness and enables you to steer your life in the right direction. By making money unnecessary, you gain the power to truly know yourself and make a positive impact not only in your own life but also in the lives of others.

Considering your current circumstances, it's crucial to establish a well-defined financial goal for yourself and commence its execution with a specific time frame in mind. You hold the power to define what you truly desire. If your current income falls short of satisfaction, aim to pursue avenues that lead you towards financial freedom. However, ensure that the path you choose aligns with your innate talents and strengths. Strive to liberate yourself from the confines of time and money, and create a multitude of options. Augment your passive income streams and build assets that will continue to benefit you in the long term.

In the unprecedented year of 2020, while many big businesses were succumbing to the challenges posed by the global pandemic, certain astute entrepreneurs were amassing great wealth. To some, this seemed puzzling, but experts understood the secret behind their success. These businessmen had wisely invested in assets that not only withstood the trials of such a demanding environment but also yielded substantial profits.

Having grasped the economic knowledge elucidated in this chapter, numerous opportunities will present themselves to you. You have the potential to further develop your expertise in this domain. However, what holds utmost importance is taking the right steps at the right time. The sooner you take action, the sooner you will attain financial freedom, allowing you to lead a life of abundance and fulfillment.

Next Step: Read this book: "Goal Setting: The Goal Setting Theory for Breakthrough Achievement and Ultimate Success - Achieve Anything You Set Your Mind To." This isn't just a book;

it's a transformative journey that reshapes your entire perspective on success. Beyond the mere act of setting goals, this guide propels you into a realm where you become the architect of your destiny. Say farewell to the stagnant patterns of the past, and usher in a future where you control the narrative of your life. Ready to transform your life through the Goal Setting Theory? You can find this book through my author profile or just visit: selfhelppowers.com/books/

CHAPTER 6
Success In Personal Life

Roger Bannister stands as a shining example of determination and the power of the human mind in the records of athletic history. In 1954, Bannister set an audacious goal for himself: to achieve the seemingly impossible feat of running a sub-four-minute mile. At that time, such a milestone had never been accomplished, leading many to doubt its feasibility. Skeptics even warned of potential dangers, suggesting that attempting to run at such an extraordinary speed could result in dire consequences, even death.

Undeterred by the prevailing doubts and naysayers, Bannister started on his relentless pursuit. For years, countless athletes endeavored to break the elusive four-minute barrier, but all efforts fell short. The world record stood stubbornly at four minutes and one second, seemingly unassailable. Gradually, even the most determined runners began to accept this limitation as an insurmountable reality.

However, Bannister knew that physical training alone would not suffice in his quest for victory. He recognized the untapped potential of his mind and realized that he needed to harness its power. Thus, he integrated visualization and imagery into his training regimen. Every day, he would vividly picture himself triumphing over the seemingly insurmountable challenge, painting a mental landscape of success. He would envision the roaring crowds, the thunderous applause, and the indescribable sensation of crossing the finish line, breaking the four-minute barrier. With each mental rehearsal, he fortified his confidence and strengthened his belief that the impossible could indeed be conquered.

Finally, in 1954, Roger Bannister shattered the four-minute mile barrier, etching his name into the records of sporting history. His achievement not only defied the doubts of others but also served as a testament to the power of unwavering belief and mental fortitude.

Yet, the story does not end there. Following Bannister's groundbreaking feat, a remarkable phenomenon unfolded. Within a year, nearly two dozen other runners surpassed the once-considered unattainable milestone. Why? It was not merely due to their physical prowess or specialized training techniques. It was the collective realization that what was once deemed impossible had been proven otherwise. Bannister's triumph ignited a spark of possibility in the hearts and minds of athletes worldwide, unleashing a wave of newfound belief and determination.

In times of personal challenges, it is all too easy to lose sight of our own potential. Yet, it is precisely during these moments that our belief becomes the pivotal key to unlocking victory. Remember, challenges may loom large until we witness someone overcome them. If others have triumphed over similar obstacles, so can you.

Even if your personal challenge appears unique and daunting, adopt it as an opportunity to set an example for others. By conquering your own difficulties, you become a beacon of inspiration and a living testament to the indomitable human spirit.

The Path to Victory in Your Personal Life

Your personal life and professional life are intricately connected, shaping your overall well-being and success. Challenges, whether they arise in your personal or professional world, have a profound impact on your entire being. It is crucial to recognize that the happiness you experience in your personal life can propel you towards triumph in your business endeavors, just as the satisfaction you achieve in your professional pursuits can enhance your personal happiness. The two aspects are inseparable, influencing each other in profound ways.

At times, personal losses can cast a long shadow, affecting not only your emotional state but also your performance in various areas of life. The profound grief that accompanies the loss of a loved one can hinder your ability to focus on your work, leading to diminished results. If the sorrow lingers, it can further exacerbate the challenges you face.

Similarly, health-related issues can emerge as formidable obstacles, impacting both your personal and professional spheres. When your well-being is compromised, it becomes increasingly challenging to find fulfillment in your personal relationships and to achieve desired success in your business endeavors. The same holds true for the dynamics within your relationships. Disharmony or discord in your close connections can hinder your ability to thrive in your professional life, no matter how determined you may be.

Therefore, when faced with challenges, it becomes imperative to give due attention to your personal life. Instead of fearing the obstacles that come your way, view them as opportunities for growth and transformation. Yes, even in your personal life, you have the power to turn challenges into opportunities. Allow me to guide you through three crucial aspects of personal life that deserve your utmost attention: peace of mind, physical health, and nurturing relationships.

In this chapter, I will dive into each of these aspects individually, shedding light on their profound influence on your personal well-being. By cultivating peace of mind, prioritizing your physical health, and fostering meaningful relationships, you can pave the way for lasting happiness in your personal life. Let's undertake this transformative journey together, delving into the importance of these three foundational aspects step by step.

I. Nurturing Your Inner Harmony

In recent times, you may have noticed that stress and depression have become prevalent topics of discussion. The growing prevalence of depression is a stark reflection of the challenges that we all face in today's world. Sometimes, the rollercoaster of personal life directly impacts your mental well-being. On other occasions, despite achieving success in your professional endeavors, you may find yourself grappling with lingering feelings of depression. To break free from the clutches of stress and attain true happiness, it is essential for you to prioritize your mental health. Achieving inner peace lays the foundation for complete fulfillment in every aspect of your life. Therefore, let's begin by focusing on nurturing your mental peace.

Earlier, we explored the significance of cultivating a positive mindset. Undoubtedly, a strong self-image significantly contributes to maintaining peace of mind. However, even in moments of mental turbulence, there exist proven methods to restore tranquility. Let us explore three of the most effective techniques without delving too deep:

1. Positive Self-Talk:

Your mind has its own language, responding to the messages you feed it. If you fill your mind with apprehensions and worries, it will continually manifest those very circumstances in your life. Hence, it is crucial to be mindful of your thoughts and the way you communicate with yourself and your loved ones. Your mind eagerly absorbs your thoughts and transforms them into reality. Your thoughts essentially amount to a conversation with yourself, which we refer to as self-communication.

Take a moment to reflect on this. Whom do you engage in the most conversations with? The answer is clear—you converse with yourself more than anyone else. Your thoughts are nothing but the words you speak to yourself. When you think, you engage in an internal dialogue, continuously shaping the mental imagery that accompanies it. The deeper these images are engraved within your mind, the longer they persist.

Recognize the immense power of your self-communication. Often, people claim that they cannot control the thoughts that enter their minds. But is that truly the case? The content of your self-communication lies entirely within your grasp.

Regardless of external circumstances, if you consistently affirm that everything will be alright, it will indeed be so. Conversely, if you allow external circumstances to sway your thoughts and convince yourself that a situation cannot be rectified, it becomes increasingly challenging to find a resolution.

The more positively you communicate with yourself, the more positivity radiates from within. Strengthening your inner self empowers you to utilize your time and energy effectively, and its transformative effects naturally manifest in your external reality.

This realization underscores that the power lies within your hands. Through your mind, you are connected to the boundless energy of nature. Yet, unless you consciously tap into this infinite reservoir, how can you expect to experience eternal happiness in life? The forces of nature can work in your favor only when you establish a deep connection with this infinite energy source.

Now that you understand the significance of engaging in positive self-communication, it is time to refine the way you speak to yourself in order to yield favorable outcomes. It is essential to cultivate a reservoir of constructive thoughts within your mind. By programming your mind with positive affirmations, you lay the groundwork for achieving the desired results.

Each person has their own unique approach to self-communication. To enhance the effectiveness of your positive self-communication, consider implementing the following techniques:

Heightened Awareness of Your Thoughts:

Begin by actively observing your thoughts. Pay close attention to the internal dialogue taking place within your mind. You may notice the presence of a self-critic, whose voice diminishes your belief in your abilities or fosters negativity in challenging situations. Take heed of this self-criticism. Whenever such thoughts arise, promptly intercept them and replace them with positive affirmations.

Establishing Distance from the "I":

There is a psychological rationale behind distancing yourself from the pronoun "I." When you say to yourself, "Why am I stressed?" It can trigger worry or self-consciousness. The term "I" directs your focus inward, preventing you from perceiving the situation objectively. To overcome this, try adopting a second- or third-person perspective. Address yourself as if you were speaking to someone else and ask, "Why are you feeling tense?" This shift in perspective enables you to gain a more accurate understanding of the situation.

Adopt Self-Motivation:

Empower yourself with inspirational words. Motivate yourself in the same way that others inspire you. Affirmations such as, "You possess remarkable qualities" or "You are capable of achieving anything" can propel you forward on your journey. Become your own source of encouragement and belief.

Cultivate Self-Acceptance:

Treat yourself as you would treat your closest friend. Adopt self-acceptance, appreciating your strengths and acknowledging areas for growth. Just as you offer unwavering support to your best friend, extend the same kindness and encouragement to yourself. Accept self-compassion and consistently treat yourself with love and respect.

Also, as previously emphasized, maintain a positive attitude. A positive attitude serves as the key to unlocking the boundless potential of your mind. It guides you through life's twists and turns, allowing you to transcend worries and forge ahead on the path to progress.

2. Unleashing the Power of Imagination:

Imagination, also known as visualization power, possesses an incredible ability to awaken your potential. By harnessing this technique, you create vivid mental images and infuse them with utmost clarity. The clearer the picture, the greater the likelihood of turning it into a reality.

Real-life examples abound, showcasing the power of imagination. Consider the legendary boxer Muhammad Ali, who spoke of envisioning himself victorious long before stepping into the ring. This mental exercise fueled him with unwavering energy, propelling him to victory.

Similarly, when Jim Carrey was a struggling young actor, he held a vision in his mind of becoming the greatest actor in the world. His vivid imagination worked its magic, ultimately propelling him to achieve greatness on the silver screen.

Michael Jordan, the basketball icon, would mentally rehearse and envision himself sinking the winning shot before ever taking it. When the moment arrived, his execution was flawless. Such perfection was attainable solely due to his unwavering imagination.

Innumerable individuals have employed the power of imagination to achieve extraordinary results. Successful people master the art of imagination, repeatedly utilizing it to manifest their desires in life. Undoubtedly, you too have witnessed instances of this phenomenon in your personal life.

Now, you may wonder how this technique functions. To grasp its workings, you must acknowledge the immense power of the mind. As you are well aware, the mind has the capacity to conceive and accomplish anything it believes possible.

Your mind readily adopts thoughts that you consistently instill within yourself and frequently repeat. Once your subconscious mind accepts these clear images, it initiates a transformation in your thinking, habits, actions, and even exposes you to new people and situations.

Thoughts possess energy, particularly focused thoughts fueled by emotional energy. These thoughts reshape the energetic landscape around us, thereby influencing the environment and inviting change.

Imagination, fueled by thought, molds your life and paves the way for success. You achieve what you dare to think. Thus, it is crucial to expand your thinking ambitiously, as doing so opens up a world brimming with opportunities and possibilities.

I would like to share some techniques to effectively harness the power of imagination. Active imagination is paramount. When you visualize, engage all your senses—touch, sound, sight, smell, and taste. Immerse yourself completely in these mental scenes, experiencing them with utmost intensity. Witness your dreams materialize as though you were watching a captivating movie, paying attention to every intricate detail.

Additionally, establish a connection with your inner self and listen to its whispers. Visualize a life that aligns with your personal desires, not the expectations of others. Honesty with yourself is paramount. Repeat your creative thoughts during self-communication.

To reinforce these messages, make it a habit to revisit these mental scenes before sleeping at night and upon waking in the morning. Many regard these times as moments of magic, as your subconscious mind is more receptive during these periods. Once you deliver your message, the subconscious mind diligently sets to work, seeking solutions on your behalf. In some instances, it yields unexpectedly astonishing results.

3. Give the necessary dose to the mind:

Just as the body thrives on nourishment, so does the mind. Just as the body gains strength and vitality from wholesome food, the mind also flourishes when fed the right sustenance. While many are mindful of their physical diet, the importance of a nourishing mental diet often goes unrecognized. In truth, the mind's diet holds greater significance than that of the body—it is an essential ingredient for overall well-being.

In simple terms, any source that brings joy to your mind and ignites a sense of mental energy and enthusiasm is considered food for the mind.

Numerous factors contribute to the mind's nourishment. Laughter, for instance, has an incredible ability to bring peace and tranquility. Engaging in hearty laughter can work wonders for the mind. Likewise, reading and immersing oneself in inspirational thoughts, exploring the life journeys and success stories of great individuals, perusing motivational books and articles, and continuously expanding one's knowledge are all forms of mental sustenance. Without providing this essential dose to the mind, it cannot operate at its full potential.

Unfortunately, in today's fast-paced world, people rarely prioritize the mental nourishment their minds require. And when they do, it often becomes an infrequent occurrence, perhaps once a month. Consequently, the mind lacks the power, energy, purpose, and constructive drive it needs to function optimally. If you desire your mind to operate at its full potential, unleashing its creativity and ingenuity, it must be fed daily. Just as you adhere to a set eating schedule for the body, the mind too requires its regular nourishment. Just as you create a dietary plan, it is crucial to establish a mental food plan.

Laughter serves as a remarkable mental supplement—an essential ingredient for a fulfilling life. Without laughter, life remains incomplete, and it serves as the finest nourishment for the mind.

Similarly, good books are a prime source of mental nourishment. Reading brings countless benefits—it enhances intelligence, fosters clarity of thought, and illuminates the path of guidance in your life.

In addition, audio and video content can provide exceptional mental sustenance. Immersing yourself in inspiring material is vital. Motivation acts as the driving force that propels your entire system forward smoothly.

You must immerse yourself in inspiration, taking advantage of living in the age of information where positive resources abound. Watch videos that resonate with you, listen to audios that uplift your spirit. Surround yourself with the things that inspire you, seeking connection with all the sources that fuel your energy.

By consciously selecting the mental food you consume, you nourish your mind and unlock its limitless potential. Just as a well-nourished body operates at its peak performance, a well-fed mind empowers you to steer life with unwavering vitality.

Finding Opportunities through Inner Peace

Deep within your quest for mental peace and your understanding of the sources of mental nourishment, a thought arises: How does this relate to creating opportunities? As you dive deeper, you'll discover that hidden within these methods and sources lie remarkable opportunities waiting to be seized.

When you walk on the path to inner peace, you align yourself with the awe-inspiring powers of nature. You gain a profound understanding of your true abilities and learn how to utilize them effectively. In fact, attaining mental peace is the gateway to unlocking the power of attraction.

The law of attraction reveals that your mind functions as a magnet within the vast universe, drawing in reality through the power of your thoughts. This concept underscores the immense impact your mindset holds over your life. Your thoughts dictate your success or failure, happiness or sorrow, prosperity or poverty. It is said that whatever your mind can conceive and hold within itself, you can truly achieve. Your thinking becomes the greatest force that shapes your reality. Finding your inner peace can truly be a driving force in drawing positive results into your life.

As you cultivate inner tranquility, you create an energetic resonance that harmonizes with the desires and goals you hold. Your peaceful mindset aligns with the frequency of abundance and propels you towards opportunities that match your aspirations.

Through the power of attraction, you attract people, circumstances, and resources that are in alignment with your deepest intentions. The peace within you becomes a magnet for favorable outcomes.

By fostering a peaceful state of mind, you develop a heightened awareness of the abundance that surrounds you. Your clarity of thought enables you to recognize opportunities that might have previously gone unnoticed. You become attuned to the subtle whispers of the universe, guiding you towards paths rich with possibilities.

Recognize your thoughts as a formidable power—an instrument capable of manifesting extraordinary outcomes. Cultivate inner peace and unleash your ability to attract the good things you seek. Allow the harmonious energy within you to draw abundance and favorable circumstances into your life. With a peaceful mindset, you open the floodgates of opportunity, propelling yourself towards a future brimming with success, joy, and fulfillment.

Revel in the transformative potential that lies within you. Discover the strength of attracting positivity through inner peace and observe the amazing opportunities that unfold on your journey.

II. Physical Health

To overcome challenges effectively, it is crucial to prioritize both your mental and physical well-being. With the emergence of various health-related challenges and the prevalence of diseases like the coronavirus, Ebola, and SARS, it becomes increasingly important to take care of your health. These conditions have disproportionately affected individuals who were physically weak or had a compromised immune system. While staying indoors may provide temporary protection from illnesses, it is not a sustainable solution. Therefore, it is vital to focus on your body and work towards strengthening your immunity.

While the topic of health is vast and can be explored in great detail, I will discuss the overall aspects of health and share ways to enhance your fitness. Here are some fundamental health considerations that everyone should bear in mind:

1. Establishing a Proper Routine and Ensuring Sufficient Energy:

Maintaining a disciplined routine is the cornerstone of good health. Waking up and sleeping at appropriate times, as well as eating meals at regular intervals, are all crucial aspects. Health flourishes through discipline, and a well-structured routine embodies discipline itself.

Physical activity is essential. While engaging in intense workouts may not be ideal for everyone, regular physical activity is necessary. One common issue is people's tendency to avoid physical activity. Many individuals delay going to the gym or make excuses due to lack of time or laziness. If you find yourself facing similar challenges, you can start with light physical activities. Walking, for instance, is an excellent form of exercise with numerous benefits. Committing to a daily walking routine can make a significant difference. Remember, even a small effort done consistently is better than doing nothing at all. Hence, strive to incorporate some physical activity into your daily routine.

2. Managing Your Weight:

Maintaining a healthy weight is vital for overall well-being. Understanding your ideal weight based on the body mass index (BMI) and keeping yourself within that range is essential. Both being overweight and being underweight can have negative effects on your health. Thus, it is important to pay attention to maintaining the right weight. Fortunately, achieving this is not overly challenging. By adopting proper eating habits and engaging in regular exercise, you can easily manage your weight.

3. Promoting an Active Lifestyle:

Encourage your body to be active throughout the day and avoid prolonged periods of sitting. Many individuals spend extended hours in a sedentary position while working. It is crucial to remember to get up periodically and move around. If possible, choose to walk for short distances instead of relying on a car for nearby errands. Additionally, consider taking the stairs instead of the elevator when feasible. By embracing an active lifestyle, you maximize your daily physical engagement and promote better health.

Prioritizing your physical health is integral to effectively cope with life's challenges. By adhering to a disciplined routine, engaging in regular physical activity, maintaining a healthy weight, and embracing an active lifestyle, you can enhance your overall well-being. Remember, even small steps towards a healthier lifestyle can have a profound impact on your life. So, seize the opportunity to take care of your body and cultivate a vibrant, resilient physical state.

4. Nourish Your Body with the Right Food Choices:

The significance of good food in maintaining your health cannot be overstated. Often, people become aware of the importance of food and beverages only when they encounter health issues. However, by cultivating a conscious approach towards nutrition, you can address and prevent numerous health-related concerns. Insufficient nutrients in your diet can significantly weaken your immune system, making it vital to incorporate foods that boost immunity into your daily meals.

5. Get optimal nutrition:

Incorporating nutrition as a crucial aspect of your daily diet provides you with remarkable benefits. Proper nutrition not only alleviates stress but also enhances your energy levels, allowing you to approach your tasks with heightened enthusiasm. Therefore, it is advisable to make a conscious decision to adopt a nutritious diet today, prioritizing your well-being instead of waiting for potential issues to arise.

For optimal nutrition, it is essential to pay attention to your dietary choices. Familiarize yourself with what you consume, understanding the reasons behind your food selections and discerning what is beneficial for your body. Oftentimes, individuals develop a habit of prioritizing taste over nutrition from a young age, neglecting the vital role that nutrition plays in overall health. However, it is crucial to prioritize nutrition above all else.

6. Get a balanced diet:

Strive to maintain a balanced diet that includes all essential elements in the appropriate quantities, tailored to your body's requirements. Three key components characterize a well-rounded diet. Firstly, choose the right carbohydrates that provide sustained energy. Secondly, incorporate sufficient protein sources into your meals. Lastly, differentiate between good fats, which are beneficial, and bad fats, which should be limited.

Ensure that your diet includes a wide range of essential nutrients. Regularly incorporate green vegetables and fresh fruits into your meals. Adopt the goodness of whole grains, legumes, and pulses. Additionally, consider including dried fruits and seeds as wholesome snacks. If you are a non-vegetarian, enjoy the benefits of lean meats like chicken and eggs. Certain types of fish rich in omega-3 fatty acids can offer remarkable advantages as well. Lastly, incorporating low-fat dairy products into your diet is beneficial for your overall well-being.

Also, there are certain food items that should be consumed in moderation. These include sugar, sweets, sugary beverages, red meat, excessive sodium, salt, and saturated fats. Additionally, it is advisable to completely avoid consuming trans fats and steer clear of alcohol and tobacco. These substances can inflict significant harm on your health, both in the short and long term.

7. Nurture Your Fitness:

Your journey to improved health begins with prioritizing fitness. Whether you aspire to enhance your physical abilities, increase strength, boost flexibility, or amplify your power, there are countless avenues through which you can elevate your fitness level. Engaging in activities like walking, swimming, cycling, weightlifting, and various sports can contribute to achieving these goals. You have the choice to train individually, join a group, or seek the guidance of a coach or trainer. However, the most crucial aspect of improving your fitness lies in cultivating an exercise habit.

Uplifting your fitness encompasses three vital components. First and foremost is stamina. Enhancing your stamina involves engaging in cardiovascular exercises that invigorate your heart. A mere 30-minute daily walk can lower levels of bad cholesterol (LDL) and subsequently reduce blood pressure. Additionally, through sweating during such activities, you can also shed unwanted weight. These exercises predominantly engage the larger muscle groups within your body.

8. Fortify your body's strength:

Next, focus on fortifying your body's strength. There are numerous methods to accomplish this goal. Strength training, in particular, targets muscle development. By partaking in strength exercises, you not only enhance muscle strength but also fortify connective tissues such as ligaments and tendons. This form of exercise also aids in maintaining bone density, facilitating your ability to endure pain and recover from injuries more effectively. Research has substantiated that higher muscle mass supports a preserved metabolic rate as you age.

The third essential aspect of fitness is flexibility. Cultivating flexibility within your body is indispensable. Flexibility entails more than simply bending your body in various directions—it encompasses activating your body to its fullest potential. Fitness experts recommend incorporating all three types of training—stamina, muscle, and flexibility—into your weekly exercise regimen. By incorporating these elements, you can enhance your fitness and establish a robust foundation for a healthy lifestyle.

Tailoring your fitness goals to suit your lifestyle is key. Some individuals thrive by visiting gyms and engaging in workouts outside their homes, while others prefer the tranquility of practicing yoga or exercise routines within their own abodes. You can choose either approach or even combine both to achieve optimal fitness outcomes.

9. Keep the continuity:

Remember, consistency is the linchpin to success. Improving your fitness level is a gradual process that unfolds over time. It is not contingent upon a single exercise or a specific diet alone. Instead, adopting a wholesome and healthy lifestyle, encompassing all these aspects, is paramount.

Attaining peak fitness might take time, and there may be moments when immediate results seem elusive. However, maintaining a regular exercise routine reaps rewards that extend beyond the physical world. Take notice of how your exercise regimen impacts your well-being. Is it reducing your stress levels and fostering harmony between your mind and body?

Rest assured, by implementing a holistic approach to fitness, you nurture your energy, continually elevate it, and empower yourself to optimize the synergy between your body and mind. Perfect fitness is a journey, and with dedication, you will unlock the ability to harness the full potential of your physical and mental capabilities.

10. Unlock the Power of Rest and Sleep:

In the hustle and bustle of today's fast-paced life, the importance of rest often gets overlooked. Many individuals strive to minimize sleep in order to maximize productivity. However, it's crucial to recognize that health operates under its own set of rules, and disregarding them can adversely affect both your mental and physical well-being.

Sleep is a natural process of rejuvenation. Just like a machine, your body cannot function incessantly—it requires periodic rest. And rest comes in the form of adequate sleep. Unfortunately, in the pursuit of squeezing more hours out of the day, people unknowingly deprive themselves of this essential restorative practice. Yet, if you genuinely wish to maximize your time and productivity, it is imperative that you prioritize obtaining sufficient sleep. The reason behind this is simple: quality sleep leaves you feeling refreshed and enables you to sustain high levels of performance over extended periods.

While the recommended amount of sleep varies according to age, experts generally advocate for a minimum of six to eight hours of sleep. Falling short of this duration is detrimental to your well-being. Consistently depriving yourself of sleep leads to the appearance of dark circles under your eyes, diminished energy levels, and persistent feelings of fatigue. Consequently, your ability to perform optimally diminishes, and life becomes more challenging.

The benefits of quality sleep are astounding. It bestows vitality upon both your body and mind, acting as a natural pain reliever. If you find yourself exhausted with lingering discomfort, a good night's sleep can offer tremendous relief. Also, quality sleep significantly impacts your mood, infusing your life with happiness and contentment.

Enhanced memory retention is another remarkable advantage of adequate sleep. Additionally, it fuels your creative potential. Upon awakening from a restful slumber, you'll find your mind brimming with fresh ideas. By harnessing the power of sleep effectively, you can unlock unprecedented levels of creative thinking.

Moreover, quality sleep serves as a shield against various ailments. Studies have shown a lower incidence of heart-related diseases among individuals who consistently obtain sufficient sleep. Also, sleep deprivation significantly contributes to increased stress levels, making it paramount to prioritize rest. Adequate sleep also fortifies your emotional resilience, instilling a profound belief in the power of your body and mind.

11. Get the Transformative Power of Yoga and Meditation:

Yoga encompasses much more than a mere physical exercise regimen. It is a profound source of mental energy and serves as the foundation for spiritual consciousness. Originating over five thousand years ago in India, yoga represents the union of mind and body. It encompasses not only physical postures but also the practice of meditation, nurturing both our physical and mental well-being.

Yoga plays a pivotal role in maintaining harmony between your body and mind. Its transformative power lies in its ability to cultivate strength and flexibility within the body, while providing an opportunity for a direct connection with the invisible power through meditation. Regular yoga practice yields remarkable benefits, aiding in the alleviation of various physical ailments such as high blood pressure, elevated cholesterol levels, and obesity. By making yoga as part of your routine, you not only shed excess weight but also sculpt a beautiful, fit physique. The beauty of yoga lies in its accessibility to everyone, with numerous techniques and postures that are easy to perform.

Pranayama, a form of yoga, involves the control and expansion of breath. By practicing proper breathing techniques, you gain mastery over prana—the vital life energy—ensuring a greater supply of oxygen to your blood and brain. Pranayama seamlessly complements various yoga asanas, combining their power to purify and discipline both the body and mind. Engaging in pranayama techniques prepares you for a deeper, more profound meditation experience.

Also, alongside asanas and pranayama, yoga encompasses the practice of mudras—hand gestures with remarkable physical and mental benefits. Regular practice of these mudras fosters balance and purity within the body and mind. Asanas not only enhance the flexibility and strength of your bones but also nurture your physical and mental prowess. Engaging in yoga facilitates the awakening of your inner energy source, paving the way for improved health and longevity. The beauty of yoga lies in its adaptability to modern lifestyles—it seamlessly integrates into our present-day routines.

Recognize that your energy serves as the key to maintaining equilibrium in all aspects of life. By cultivating and harnessing your inner energy, you accelerate your journey toward happiness and success. The more you nurture and invigorate yourself, the greater your capacity to achieve fulfillment in every facet of your life.

Finding Opportunities within Physical Fitness

You possess a profound understanding of the hidden opportunities that lie within physical health. Health stands as the cornerstone of human existence. Without it, the pleasures of life, such as wealth, entertainment, luxury, and comforts, pale in comparison. No matter the abundance of monetary riches, they hold little value without good health. While money can be regained if lost, the same cannot be said for health—it is an irreplaceable treasure.

Recognizing the importance of good health is essential for a successful life. As we all know that a successful life encompasses three dimensions: health, wealth, and happiness. It is crucial that all three facets stand equally robust.

Remember, a healthy body and a healthy mind are interconnected. Thus, it is imperative to prioritize both mental and physical well-being. The stronger you become, the better equipped you are to tackle challenges head-on, pouring your full energy into seizing every available opportunity.

A healthy body empowers you to transcend limits, enabling you to accomplish feats once deemed impossible. It grants you the resilience to endure and the vitality to thrive. Meanwhile, a healthy mind serves as a wellspring of creativity, focus, and clarity. It empowers you to steer the intricacies of life with unwavering determination and a positive outlook.

When your physical and mental health harmoniously intertwine, you unleash your full potential. You become a force to be reckoned with, capable of surmounting any obstacle that comes your way. By investing in your well-being, you invest in a brighter future—one filled with boundless opportunities waiting to be seized.

III. Emotional happiness

Emotional happiness stands as a pivotal element in each individual's life, significantly impacting mental serenity and physical well-being. The core essence of emotional happiness lies within the relationships you cultivate with yourself. In this section, we will explore the profound importance of emotional happiness and the role relationships play as the third crucial aspect of your personal journey.

Be it your personal or professional life, the quality of your relationships serves as a determining factor in your overall happiness and triumphs. In your professional journey, cultivating positive connections promotes career growth, and in your personal life, it nurtures inner peace. By maintaining a well-balanced personal life, you effortlessly extend that equilibrium to your professional endeavors. Establishing solid relationships with colleagues, business partners, distributors, investors, and customers simplifies your work, optimizing both time and energy utilization. Likewise, fostering strong bonds with your life partner, family, children, friends, relatives, and neighbors envelops you with an inner radiance, ensuring efficient allocation of your invaluable resources.

Throughout the stages of life, certain individuals cross our paths, irrevocably transforming our trajectories. Indeed, people are indispensable components of our success. Imagine excelling in all areas of life, only to be surrounded by individuals who consistently emit negativity and demoralize your aspirations. In such circumstances, channeling your full energy towards success becomes an arduous task. Even a mere hint of doubt can veer you away from your path. Similarly, in your quest for acquiring new knowledge, learning from individuals lacking expertise in the subject matter will impede your progress. The significance of selecting the right person transcends both personal and professional spheres, shaping the course of your journey.

People hold immense significance in everyone's lives. Certain individuals leave an indelible mark, altering the very fabric of our existence. The encounters, observations, and conversations with such individuals possess the power to steer our lives in new directions. Imagine the possibilities if you were surrounded by numerous positive souls who exude inspiration and support. With their presence, you would possess the fortitude to achieve anything your heart desires.

As you traverse the path to success, remain mindful of the company you keep. Take a moment to evaluate your current situation. Who are the individuals standing by your side today? Who are your companions on this journey? Do they infuse your life with positivity, or do they sow seeds of negativity? Are they aiding you in reaching your goals, or are they diverting you from your intended path?

Negativity, although enticing in its allure, possesses a unique magnetism that draws people toward it. Straying from your goals is a simple feat, while staying resolute on the path to success demands unwavering commitment. Therefore, endeavor to surround yourself with individuals who inspire you to progress. Keep company with those who steadfastly support you, even in the face of adversity. Recognize that detaching from someone detrimental to your well-being need not always involve confrontation. Gradually, you can create distance between yourself and negative influences, simultaneously gravitating towards positive influences.

A positive person radiates self-assurance, remaining undeterred by external opinions. Confronted with any situation, they maintain an unwavering smile. Such individuals not only transform their own lives but also become catalysts for change in the lives of others. Strive to embody the qualities of such a person and seek out their presence in your own life.

Surrounding yourself with positive individuals forms a crucial cornerstone for your personal growth. In their presence, you will consistently discover new avenues of learning and ignite a passionate drive towards your goals. Even during moments of stumbling, rest assured that nearby companions will lend their support, guiding you back on track. By fostering harmonious relationships in your personal life, you will harness a wellspring of happiness, infusing vitality into your professional endeavors.

Mastering the art of relationship-building is a profound social skill, requiring a delicate balance of effective communication and charismatic personality. Every day, you encounter numerous individuals, cross paths with influential figures, and frequent locations brimming with opportunities. Regrettably, should you choose to merely observe from a distance, you unknowingly relinquish golden chances for connection. Remember, golden opportunities seldom present themselves repeatedly. Hence, whenever you encounter such moments, seize them wholeheartedly. Positive and supportive individuals are indispensable across all aspects of life.

In this era of information and connectivity, we possess an abundance of means to connect with others. Remain attentive to individuals whom you aspire to connect with, identifying those who hold the potential to contribute to your success. At times, you may require guidance, cooperation, inspiration, or assistance in diverse forms. It is the people that elevate businesses to greatness, and leaders become truly remarkable due to their alliances. Consider yourself fortunate should you find numerous individuals willing to stand by your side, even amidst challenging circumstances. You, too, have the potential to attract such invaluable allies.

Invest wisely in nurturing relationships. Strong bonds alleviate the burdens of life, propelling you forward at each step of your journey. Our social environment flourishes when we surround ourselves with like-minded individuals, fostering an atmosphere of growth and progress. As previously mentioned, residing among individuals who harbor ambitious dreams and adopt the pursuit of advancement significantly impacts your personal development.

Likewise, emotional resilience serves as a vital attribute during life's many twists and turns. During such moments, close relationships prove invaluable. No matter how vast an individual's knowledge may be, they inevitably seek support when emotionally fragile. In these instances, having steadfast relationships becomes an invaluable asset. Without such unwavering support systems, one may unknowingly expose themselves to exploitation. During times of emotional vulnerability, it is crucial to surround yourself with individuals who genuinely understand and empathize with your experiences.

Building strong relationships necessitates investment—both in terms of time and effort. Relationships operate on the unspoken principle of reciprocity. Merely expecting others to invest in you while neglecting your own contributions leads to unfulfilled expectations. Instead, endeavor to enhance the lives of those around you, making them feel cherished and valued. Express your appreciation to individuals whom you hold dear. The deeper your understanding of others, the deeper their understanding of you becomes.

Building relationships may be relatively straightforward, but maintaining them poses a formidable challenge. Relationships are fragile, tethered by a delicate thread. Straining it too much will cause it to snap, while neglecting it leaves room for it to slip away. Thus, nurturing coordination and balance remains paramount.

Investing in relationships yields long-term dividends, particularly during times of genuine need. Additionally, the happiness derived from fostering personal connections permeates and elevates various spheres of life.

Allocate ample time to your relationships. Treasure quality moments with your loved ones as a pivotal factor in nurturing strong bonds, fostering love, connection, and unity within your family. By dedicating quality time to your family, you equip them with the tools to confront challenges, instill a sense of security, uphold cherished family values, and instill unwavering confidence in children. The rewards of investing time in your relationships extend far beyond mere satisfaction—they shape the very fabric of a fulfilling and purposeful life.

Spending quality time with your family holds immense significance as it cultivates deep-rooted relationships and strengthens the bonds that tie you together. Often, individuals, especially children, seek acceptance and a sense of belonging among friends and social circles. However, it is within the family unit that they find a profound sense of togetherness, security, and the freedom to express themselves.

One of the compelling reasons to prioritize family time is the invaluable opportunity it provides for heartfelt conversations. Within the family, individuals can freely share their emotions, knowing they will be heard and understood without judgment. This nurturing environment enables them to celebrate their achievements and find solace during challenging times, surrounded by loved ones who genuinely rejoice in their success.

Sadly, the modern world often strains family connections, causing heartfelt interactions to dwindle. The precious wisdom once effortlessly transmitted within the family unit has become less accessible. While today's children have access to a wealth of educational resources, it remains crucial to allocate dedicated family time for meaningful discussions, where problems and life situations can be openly addressed and resolved. This fosters a deeper understanding of life's complexities, equipping them with essential life skills.

Special occasions and festive celebrations serve as beacons of unity, contentment, and inner security within the family. Each interaction, whether it's a warm greeting, bidding farewell, sharing meals, or simply spending quality time together, contributes to the creation of cherished family traditions. Commemorating birthdays, wedding anniversaries, and festivals collectively helps to preserve and reinforce these treasured customs, forging lasting memories.

Moreover, the atmosphere you cultivate within your family unit extends beyond its boundaries, influencing your connection with the wider society. Your family members are your cherished companions, with whom you can create an environment of joy and fulfillment, radiating happiness throughout your lives.

Deep down, everyone yearns for the warmth and connectedness that family provides. If such opportunities are scarce, it falls upon you to create them. Numerous avenues exist for you to engage in quality time with your loved ones. Consider sharing at least one meal together each day, whether it's breakfast or dinner. This shared experience serves as a precious moment for everyone to come together, sharing thoughts, and building stronger bonds. During this time, ensure that electronic distractions such as television are set aside, allowing for undivided attention and meaningful conversation.

Also, explore daily or weekly activities that can be enjoyed collectively, such as exercising together, reading together, taking walks, or engaging in household chores as a team. By seeking out opportunities that bring everyone together, you will discover countless moments to foster unity and nurture relationships. Additionally, prioritize going on family vacations at regular intervals, despite the challenges of aligning everyone's schedules. These occasions provide invaluable opportunities to create lifelong memories and reinforce the importance of family in your lives.

Recognize the profound significance of love in your journey. Love forms the bedrock of personal relationships, exerting its greatest impact during trying times. Just as oxygen sustains your mind and body, love acts as an indispensable life force. There is no alternative. The more deeply you nurture your connections with love, the more robust your physical and emotional well-being becomes. Love serves as a potent antidote to stress, acting as the ultimate antidepressant. Therefore, cherish and openly express your love for your partner. The happiness derived from love empowers you to conquer any challenge life presents.

Opportunity Hidden in Emotional Happiness

Opportunity can often be found concealed within the depths of emotional happiness. It is said that true relationships reveal themselves during times of adversity, and you have likely experienced this truth firsthand. Indeed, there is wisdom in the age-old adage that suggests testing individuals in challenging circumstances. These words continue to hold their weight in the present day.

In the face of personal challenges, it is an opportune moment to discern the authenticity of your relationships. Take note of those who steadfastly stand by your side, offering unwavering support during difficult times. Beware of those who make empty claims of loyalty only to turn away when you need them the most. True support extends beyond mere financial assistance; emotional backing holds the utmost significance.

Likewise, moments of adversity present an extraordinary opportunity for love relationships to flourish. During the unprecedented lockdowns of the 2020 pandemic, two distinct reactions emerged. While some couples found themselves engaging in senseless arguments, others experienced a remarkable transformation in their relationships. This divergence arose from perceiving the situation as an opportunity rather than an obstacle. The enforced isolation became a golden chance to reconnect and spend quality time together. Strengthened bonds emerged within families, and long-forgotten connections were revived through heartfelt conversations. Amidst the hardship that many lamented, numerous individuals seized the occasion to fortify their personal networks.

When individuals carve out time amidst their demanding lives to be with their loved ones, they emerge emotionally fortified. Such experiences create a resilience that renders subsequent challenges less impactful. Moreover, emotional strength permeates every facet of your life. Therefore, from this day forward, invest in nurturing your emotional well-being. Cultivate its strength and harness this newfound power to infuse your life with happiness.

Discover the immense power that resides within emotional happiness. Acknowledge the invaluable support that arises during challenging times, and cherish the relationships that endure through adversity. By doing so, you will not only enhance your personal growth but also uncover the limitless joy that emanates from a resilient and fulfilled life.

CHAPTER 7
Your Complete Security System

Some challenges in life may appear insurmountable at first glance. They defy an immediate solution, yet when confronted head-on, they create opportunities for success that can impact many lives. Such a challenge emerged in the early days of this century, when the world was faced with a seemingly unsolvable problem.

Before the year 2000, a crisis loomed over the global computer communication system. A problem so significant that it was believed to potentially bring computers to a halt. Although it may seem trivial to contemplate now, at the time, it presented a grave predicament, casting an unprecedented shadow over the world.

This predicament was none other than the infamous 'Y2K' bug. You may have come across this term before, but let's dive deeper into what it entailed. In the early stages of electronic computing, computer systems worldwide utilized only two digits to represent the year. The 'Y' in 'Y2K' symbolized the year, while '2K' represented the year 2000. As the year 1999 drew to a close, computer systems faced a daunting challenge—they were unable to transition to the year beyond December 31, 1999. Although the date and month could be adjusted for the upcoming year, the first two digits of the year remained fixed. Consequently, when January 1, 2000 arrived, computer screens displayed the date as 01/01/1900, a hundred years in the past. This anomaly came to be known as the 'Y2K bug' or the 'Millennium Bug'—a flaw in computer coding.

Computer systems in the United States and Europe had not accounted for the year 2000 and beyond. For instance, all computer calculations in America adhered to the month-day-year format, with only two-digit representation for the year. Therefore, as 1999 transitioned to 2000, all dates would have appeared as 01-01-00, effectively setting the clock back a century. The repercussions of this oversight were immense.

Experts in the field warned that the lack of adequate programs for the 21st century could lead to the collapse of computer systems. Critical computer programs, vital for the functioning of the economy, were at risk of failure. This scenario could trigger a multitude of problems simultaneously. Banks might be unable to process checks or transfers, governments would struggle with their daily operations, and power grids could fail, disrupting essential services such as transportation and water supply. Embedded processors in various devices, including elevators, printers, and navigation systems, could malfunction. Businesses would suffer due to declining sales and production. ATMs and banks would face severe disruptions, potentially causing a complete economic collapse. The repercussions extended to all computerized systems, including vital sectors like banking and healthcare, leading to potential chaos.

As panic ensued and normal activities faced derailing consequences, European and American companies sought a solution to this crisis. The dire need for a new date framework that could adapt to the changing years gradually became evident. However, achieving such a transformation required a significant overhaul of computer infrastructure, necessitating the expertise of a vast number of skilled computer engineers. Accomplishing this feat seemed nearly impossible within the available time frame. Yet, in the face of adversity, Indian engineers courageously accepted the responsibility of tackling this unprecedented challenge.

India had already established IT powerhouses like Infosys and Wipro, ready to adopt and harness the global talent pool of IT professionals. No other nation possessed such a vast reserve of skilled labor at affordable rates. This unique advantage compelled the attention of American and European companies to turn towards India. In this crucial time, it was the ambitious and skilled youth of India who rose to the occasion, showcasing their exceptional abilities on the world stage.

Undoubtedly, an immense number of resources was invested in resolving the 'Y2K' bug. Estimates suggest that a staggering 200 to 300 billion US dollars were spent over a five-year period to rectify the issue. Some experts even project the total cost to have reached an astronomical figure ranging from 600 to 1,600 billion US dollars.

During this critical phase, numerous Indian software companies dedicated themselves to solving the 'Y2K' bug. Their efforts catapulted the Indian tech industry to unprecedented heights, seemingly unstoppable. India's IT and services exports, which commenced in 1999, soared to record-breaking levels in the subsequent years. It is estimated that approximately 40 percent of the total revenue of Indian tech companies at that time was derived from contracts secured to address the 'Y2K' bug on behalf of foreign enterprises.

IIS Infotech, renowned for its expertise, successfully rewrote code to ensure software compliance with the 'Y2K' standards. They were entrusted with critical projects by esteemed overseas clients, including Citibank, American Express, G.E., and prominent American companies such as Prudential. Indian software companies played a pivotal role in assisting most advanced nations in transitioning smoothly from the 20th century to the 21st century, resolving the infamous 'Y2K' bug. This significant achievement led to other notable companies like Microsoft and IBM outsourcing similar work to Indian firms. The interdependence between organizations further solidified the growing partnership between India and America, strengthening Indo-American relations.

During the 'Y2K' bug frenzy, Indian computer engineers emerged as problem solvers, diligently resolving issues across the United States. Their expertise was sought after not only by American hospitals and companies but also by various global entities. At that time, around 1.5 million Indian engineers were diligently serving in America. Not only did Indian companies amass substantial revenue from these endeavors, but the 'Y2K' episode also propelled them into the international market, securing their position as industry leaders in the present day.

Today, when the world marvels at the prowess of Indian IT engineers, we must acknowledge that their triumph over the 'Y2K' bug played a significant role. By seizing this challenge as an opportunity, Indian IT engineers paved the way for their compatriots to assume influential positions in leading IT companies such as Google and Microsoft.

This incredible tale serves as a testament to turning the impossible into reality. Often, what may initially appear insurmountable holds immense potential for growth and success. The emergence of such a remarkable opportunity opened doors for Indian engineers, showcasing their extraordinary capabilities while providing a pathway for others to progress.

Method of turning challenges into opportunities

Throughout this book, we have dived deep into various aspects of personal and professional growth. We have explored the significance of cultivating a resilient mindset, setting ambitious goals, and harnessing the potential of challenges to create new opportunities. In essence, we have been building a system—a framework designed to strengthen you. My aim is not only to equip myself with the tools to overcome present obstacles but also to ensure that future challenges have minimal impact on your path to success.

We have discussed numerous techniques and approaches for personal and professional excellence. Whether it is developing a growth mindset, crafting strategic goals, or navigating the worlds of success in both your personal and professional life, the methods we have explored are powerful enough to conquer any challenge and unlock a world of new possibilities. However, it is understandable that despite having access to these valuable insights, many individuals may struggle to effectively implement them.

It's akin to having all the components of a well-assembled machine but being uncertain of how to set it in motion. This dilemma is something that numerous people encounter—it's a part of the journey. Therefore, it is crucial that we now reveal the method that will not only set your machine in motion but also ensure it never comes to a halt. This method forms a cohesive system that, once mastered, empowers you to leverage every technique effectively.

This system acts as a guiding compass, directing you towards optimal utilization of the knowledge and skills you have acquired. It provides a roadmap to seamlessly integrate these transformative strategies into your daily life. With this system in place, you will not only experience immediate breakthroughs but also develop the ability to steer any challenge that comes your way with grace and ease.

System Of Habit

Habits—they govern our lives. We are all entwined in the web of various habits. But have you ever considered that a habit can be a system in itself? In its true essence, a habit is a system that empowers you to utilize every method at your disposal. Let's dive deeper into this concept.

A habit is a recurring pattern of behavior that becomes ingrained in a person's natural response to a given situation. Some habits are positive, such as taking a daily one-kilometer walk, while others are negative, like smoking during breaks. When we face stress, our negative behavioral habits tend to amplify. That is why it is crucial to cultivate good habits and eliminate detrimental ones. Any task that becomes a habit becomes easier to accomplish.

To understand the process of habits, let's consider the example of learning to drive a car for the first time. In the initial stages, you are cautious and meticulous, aware of each action—when to depress the clutch, change gears, apply brakes, hold the steering wheel, honk the horn, and more. All your senses are actively engaged in this learning process. You observe keenly, listen attentively, smell the surroundings, communicate effectively, and maintain a firm grip on the wheel. Essentially, you perform every action with utmost consciousness. As your senses actively learn, a clear message is relayed to your mind. Initially, you meticulously handle each aspect of driving. However, what happens after a few weeks or months of daily practice? You no longer pay close attention to every detail. Your feet effortlessly steer the pedals, and you steer leisurely. You reach your destination comfortably, effortlessly. What was once challenging gradually becomes second nature.

This is the essence of habit formation. At first glance, everything in life appears daunting. But as you consciously engage in an activity, it gradually becomes effortless. Take a moment to examine your daily routine—you will discover numerous tasks that you effortlessly perform. You steer your room even in your sleep, finding your way to the bathroom or locating the switch in the darkness. You accomplish tasks through intuition and familiarity. When you program your mind effectively, anything is possible.

How long does it take for habits to solidify? There is a popular belief that "if you continuously do something for 21 days, it becomes a habit." While this notion may hold some truth, there is no universal standard of 21 days for everyone. The time required to form a habit varies. Some individuals may take a few days, weeks, months, or even years. It all depends on your determination. If you are truly committed to transforming your life, a few weeks or months will suffice.

There is another intriguing aspect of habits—they attract other habits of a similar nature. Often, adopting one bad habit leads to the acquisition of several others. Conversely, cultivating a positive habit spawns a cascade of other beneficial habits. For instance, if you develop a fitness routine, you naturally become more mindful of your dietary choices and overall health. A single fitness habit can trigger the development of numerous related habits. Simply put, you just need to take the first step, and the rest will follow effortlessly.

Build your System on the Mechanism of Habits

To achieve your goals, you must adopt good habits. Creating new positive habits or replacing negative ones requires intentional and consistent practice of a new behavior until it becomes automatic, seamlessly woven into the fabric of your daily life.

The level of your desire and commitment will determine the speed of change. Dedicate yourself to practicing the desired habit relentlessly, repeating the process over and over until it becomes second nature. Habits are the keys to effective execution—they establish a system that makes every task easier to accomplish. They are the bridge between intention and action.

Good habits pave the clear path to success. If you have set a goal but find yourself struggling to find the right way to reach it, take a moment to reflect. Consider the habits that successful individuals who have achieved similar goals possess. What habits do they adopt that you may be lacking? Recognize the power of adopting good habits. If there are any detrimental habits hindering your progress, replace them with positive alternatives. This is a practical solution. Repeat the process consistently, and watch as these actions evolve into deeply ingrained habits.

Imagine building your very own security system—a system constructed with a network of habits. In ancient times, Gautam Buddha preached his teachings to disciples and devotees every day. He shared formulas for attaining happiness and peace in life. People would come, listen attentively, express their gratitude, and depart. One of Buddha's disciples pondered why only a few individuals seemed to truly benefit from these teachings while others did not.

Curiosity piqued, the disciple approached Buddha and asked the reason behind this disparity. Buddha smiled upon hearing the question and replied, "If someone asks you for directions to the palace, but despite your guidance, they veer off course, what can you do?" The disciple pondered for a moment and responded, "My role is solely to provide guidance. If they choose to stray, there is little I can do to prevent it."

Buddha nodded in agreement and said, "You have found your answer. My purpose is to enlighten people, to shed light on the distinction between right and wrong. It is up to individuals to decide whether to adopt these teachings in their lives. Those who integrate these sutras find welfare, happiness, and peace. Those who neglect them continue to wander."

You hold the knowledge and the way forward. It is your responsibility to tread the path with unwavering determination. If you veer off course, no one else can be held accountable. Today, in this very moment, initiate the change within your life. You are the architect of your own security system. Craft a magnificent blueprint for your journey and commence the execution. The sooner you take those initial steps, the sooner you will find yourself at your desired destination.

Believe in the power of habits, for they possess the potential to transform your life. Adopt the change, adopt the journey, and become the master of your destiny. The road ahead may be challenging, but as you persist and integrate positive habits into your daily routine, you will witness the astounding transformation that unfolds within you.

So, you know the way, it is your job to walk on it. If you go astray, no one else can be responsible for it. So, start the change in your life today and from now itself. You have to build your own security system. Make a grand plan for yourself and start executing on it. The sooner you start walking, the sooner you will reach your goal.

CHAPTER 8
A Look at The Important Points

When faced with a challenge today, how do you perceive it? Is it an insurmountable obstacle or a potential opportunity? Perhaps what you perceive as a mere challenge holds within it a hidden treasure, waiting to be unearthed.

To boldly assert that "every challenge is a great opportunity" requires immense courage, both to acknowledge and to apply in your life's journey. Challenges are an inevitable part of our existence, yet within each challenge lies the seed of a solution. This is the fundamental law of creation, perpetually manifesting itself in various forms.

What are the challenges?

Necessity births invention, emptiness sparks creation, and change propels the world forward. Every passing moment brings forth new circumstances, often accompanied by challenges. Yet, you possess the extraordinary ability not only to overcome these challenges but also to seize the opportunities they present.

Amidst the vast landscape of challenges, solutions abound. However, it is crucial to cultivate the right perspective—a lens that enables you to discern the hidden opportunities amidst the apparent hurdles. While many individuals remain preoccupied with perceiving only the challenges, you have the power to perceive the untapped potential concealed within each one.

Attitude serves as the compass that guides your path. If you choose to view circumstances through a distorted lens, the way forward will remain obscured. Conversely, when your perspective aligns with the truth of the matter, you will begin to perceive opportunities even amidst the most formidable challenges.

Nature, too, imparts its wisdom by challenging us rather than allowing us to flee. It presents us with the chance to evolve, to grow stronger through the crucible of adversity. Should we shy away from challenges or seek refuge from them, we would forego the invaluable gifts bestowed upon us by nature itself.

Indeed, encountering challenges is an inherent aspect of life, essential for its very meaning. These hurdles serve as catalysts, infusing vitality and vigor into your being. Throughout the annals of human civilization, cultures that adopted and surmounted challenges emerged stronger, while those built on foundations devoid of challenges have faded into obscurity.

The benefits of embracing challenges are manifold. Firstly, challenges illuminate the depth of your inner strength, unveiling reservoirs of fortitude you may have never realized existed.

Secondly, challenges instill a profound sense of gratitude, reminding you of the blessings that often go unnoticed amidst the trials.

Also, challenges clarify your true desires and aspirations, providing clarity and direction in your pursuit of a meaningful life.

Challenges cultivate qualities such as determination, patience, and resilience, allowing you to steer future obstacles with greater ease.

Likewise, challenges ignite the fires of creativity, unlocking innovative solutions and fostering personal growth. Lastly, it is through overcoming challenges that your accomplishments acquire a profound sense of fulfillment and significance.

Background of Challenges

Within the challenges lie profound opportunities, awaiting those courageous individuals who refuse to shy away but instead conquer them. Your life, too, is a book with tales of triumph over adversity. As you reflect upon your own journey, you'll discover that the remarkable stories that grace your life's narrative are often born from the crucible of challenges.

Challenges possess an innate capacity to metamorphose into opportunities, governed by a remarkable system that awaits your understanding. However, before delving into the intricacies of this system, it is essential to grasp the concept of your relationship with challenges and why they may unsettle you.

Security, a fundamental pursuit of human nature, holds a prominent place in our lives. Since time immemorial, humanity has regarded security as a paramount need. When the foundations of our perceived security are shaken, even the slightest disruption triggers unease, perceived as a challenge or problem.

Similarly, humans are predisposed to resist change. The prevailing sentiment often questions the necessity of altering a state of affairs when everything seems to be flowing smoothly. Yet, deep within our collective consciousness, we recognize change as an immutable law of the universe. Every passing moment bears witness to ceaseless transformation, for without it, progress and evolution would stagnate.

Challenges manifest in various forms and may encompass a broad spectrum of experiences. Broadly categorized, challenges can be classified into five distinct domains: personal, emotional, health-related, financial, and untimely challenges. However, succumbing to distress or anxiety in the face of these challenges provides no solution. Prolonged turmoil engenders a multitude of problems, serving as a breeding ground for depression. Mental and physical afflictions ensue, inevitably impacting both personal and professional aspects of life.

Allowing challenges to debilitate you serves no purpose. In fact, enduring distress for prolonged periods can compound your troubles. Also, the repercussions extend beyond your own well-being and seep into the lives of those around you. Recognize that embracing challenges head-on is the key, swiftly seeking resolution when adversity strikes. By doing so, you prevent the escalation of further complications.

The path to resolution lies neither in the sorrows of the past nor in the anxieties of the future. True solace resides in the present moment—the only tangible reality. The present holds infinite potential, devoid of any influence from the past or future. Direct your focus towards the present, for it encompasses the entirety of your existence. While the lessons gleaned from past experiences are invaluable, they serve as guiding beacons to steer the present. Likewise, contemplating the future serves a purpose only insofar as it enables effective planning for present actions.

Regardless of the magnitude of a challenge, its solution invariably resides in the present moment. This unwavering mantra reveals itself upon delving deep into the heart of challenges. Consider the woven fabric of your life, and you may discover moments when what appeared to be unfortunate events ultimately turned out to be significant blessings. Initially, you may resist certain circumstances, but in due time, you realize that without those very experiences, you would have missed out on invaluable opportunities.

This is the essence of our existence. Life, with its intricate interplay of events, harbors a multitude of possibilities, even amidst seemingly unfavorable circumstances. By adopting a positive outlook, you tap into the hidden potential within every challenge, revealing the gifts that are waiting for you to discover.

Positive Mind System

Deep within you lie extraordinary abilities, waiting to be realized amidst a sea of dormant potential. Instead of succumbing to the influence of weak-minded individuals, you have the power to rise above and illuminate the path for yourself and others. It all begins with recognizing the strength of your self-image, for within it lies the key to transforming challenges into opportunities.

Every individual harbors a mental image of themselves, shaped by thoughts and beliefs. This self-image encompasses your physical, emotional, social, spiritual, and cognitive aspects of being. It is the lens through which you perceive yourself. If your self-image is weak, it becomes the breeding ground for a feeble mindset, hindering your ability to confront even the simplest of challenges. Therefore, cultivating a robust self-image becomes paramount in establishing a system that converts challenges into stepping stones towards success.

Your mind operates akin to a sophisticated computer system, programmed to function in specific ways. Without awareness of this programming process, you relinquish control over your life's course. However, as you become conscious of this intricate mechanism, you naturally regain command over your destiny.

Transform your attitude towards challenges and adopt the mindset of a victor. Begin by identifying the crux of your problem. Write it down, allowing clarity to illuminate your path. By gaining a clear understanding of the challenges you face, you empower yourself to make informed choices about how to respond.

The human mind gravitates towards simplicity. To steer uncertainty and ambiguity, it is essential to observe your reactions and reframe negative responses into positive ones. By embracing this transformative shift, you unlock a wealth of solutions to your problems.

Preconceived notions often plague individuals, becoming the catalyst for many of life's quandaries. Individuals frequently ruminate over perceived problems long before they materialize, fostering a cycle of negative thinking. Yet, by breaking free from the bonds of prejudice, you liberate yourself from countless self-imposed predicaments.

Mistakes are an inherent part of the human experience. However, it is your reaction to these missteps that often exacerbates the problem. Instead of fleeing from errors or lamenting over them, the most powerful approach is to extract valuable lessons and forge ahead, armed with newfound wisdom.

Develop an impenetrable mental armor to shield yourself from challenges. By doing so, you repel negativity and attract positive forces into your life. Your decisions become grounded in active thinking, bolstering your confidence and propelling you towards your goals with ease.

Deepen your emotional understanding. Cultivate a reservoir of positive feelings, while diminishing negative ones. Mastery over emotions lies in harnessing the power of positive emotions and minimizing the impact of negative ones.

Resolve challenges first in your mind. Challenges are an inevitable part of life's journey. However, there is no benefit in wallowing in worry. By shifting your focus towards seeking solutions, you liberate yourself from the clutches of anxiety. Adopt the belief that, no matter the obstacle, you possess the innate capacity to find a solution.

Your Winning Strategy

No matter how daunting the circumstances may seem, and no matter how many challenges surround you, remember that you possess the power to remain unscathed. It all begins with your unwavering determination and an upgraded strategy to steer through challenging times.

To transform your challenges into golden opportunities, you need to establish strong and compelling goals. Without a clear plan, a robust action strategy, and well-defined objectives, progress becomes arduous. Even in the face of the toughest challenges, goal setting wields its enchanting power. With a slight recalibration of your strategy, remarkable outcomes await you.

When you set meaningful goals for yourself, you assume accountability for your actions. Rather than merely engaging in idle contemplation, you adopt the practice of taking purposeful steps. The beauty of this process lies in the continual improvement of your efficiency.

By employing the time-tested principle of goal setting, you can achieve any objective, be it financial or personal in nature. Breaking down your goals into smaller, manageable parts makes even the loftiest aspirations more attainable. Adopt the power of clarity as you define your goals, establish deadlines, and forge ahead. In times of challenge, redefining old goals and creating new ones allows you to forge a path of progress.

Once your goals are redefined, it is crucial to ensure their implementation. This entails charting out actionable steps that will propel you towards your desired outcomes. When you declare your unwavering commitment to a goal, you are wholeheartedly dedicated to its successful realization.

The trajectory of your life, whether it be marked by triumph or failure, hinges upon your ability to make sound decisions. The timeliness and quality of your choices significantly influence the speed at which you journey towards success. Effective time management enables you to alleviate the burden of indecision, empowering you to make timely and informed choices.

Success in Professional Life

In the professional world, challenges often present themselves as hidden opportunities awaiting your action. By taking decisive steps forward, you unlock the door to these opportunities, allowing them to manifest naturally.

An integral part of this process involves assessing your current challenges and using them as stepping stones to new possibilities. Keep in mind that your specific challenges will vary based on your unique circumstances, and the corresponding opportunities will arise accordingly.

Establishing yourself as an expert holds tremendous value in the eyes of others. Whether you're employed, self-employed, or engaged in business ventures, positioning yourself as an authority is paramount. People naturally gravitate towards those with expertise, seeking their guidance, products, or services. During challenging times, this demand for experts only intensifies, while those lacking specialized knowledge may find themselves overlooked.

Equipping yourself with economic knowledge is vital for navigating economic challenges effectively. A solid understanding of financial principles not only guides you towards earning money the right way but also empowers you to make wise investment decisions, maximizing your returns.

To achieve victory on the financial front, it is essential to assess your current financial standing. Begin by understanding your existing sources of income and evaluating their suitability for your long-term goals.

Regardless of your income source, everyone desires financial security, as it plays a pivotal role in one's mental well-being.

True wealth lies in the balance between your assets and liabilities. Assets generate income, adding money to your pocket, while liabilities drain your resources. Striving for prosperity necessitates finding the optimal combination of assets and liabilities. To overcome long-term financial challenges, focus on reducing liabilities and increasing your assets.

Establishing a stream of income that doesn't solely rely on your active involvement is crucial. Passive income offers a potent solution in this regard. By strategically working towards building assets and generating passive income, you pave the way to financial abundance and ultimately attain financial freedom.

Success in Personal Life

When you encounter challenges in your personal life, they may initially appear insurmountable. However, remember that you are not the first person to face such obstacles. Many individuals have overcome similar trials before you. And if your challenge happens to be unique, even better! By conquering it, you not only triumph over adversity but also become an inspiration for others.

Your personal and professional lives are interconnected. Finding happiness in your personal life not only breeds success in business but also fosters personal fulfillment. Likewise, personal unhappiness can lead to failure in business, and business setbacks can adversely affect your personal well-being. These worlds are intricately linked.

The mind possesses its own language and operates according to the messages you feed it. If you constantly fill your mind with apprehension and worry, it will continuously attract those same experiences into your life. Hence, it is crucial to be mindful of your thoughts.

Your mind readily accepts the thoughts that you consistently instill within yourself and repeat frequently. When your subconscious mind adopts these clear mental images, it starts shaping your thoughts, habits, actions, and even introduces you to new people and situations.

Just as the body requires nourishment, the mind also needs its own sustenance. Just as the body thrives on nutritious food, the mind flourishes when fed with positive stimuli. Any source that pleases your mind and energizes you mentally is nourishment for the mind.

Striving for inner peace allows you to tap into the wondrous powers of nature and recognize your true potential. It enables you to unleash your abilities and utilize them to their fullest extent. Achieving mental peace is also the key to unlocking the power of attraction.

Both mental and physical health are essential for effectively navigating life's challenges. With the emergence of various health-related issues and diseases, it is vital to prioritize your well-being.

Your energy levels play a significant role in maintaining balance in your life. The more you cultivate and harness your energy, the greater your capacity to attain happiness and success at an accelerated pace.

The connection between a healthy body and a healthy mind is profound. Therefore, it is crucial to prioritize both your mental and physical well-being. Strengthening yourself holistically empowers you to confront challenges head-on and invest your full energy into seizing every available opportunity.

Emotional happiness holds immense importance in anyone's life. It not only impacts your mental tranquility but also influences your physical health. Building fulfilling relationships with yourself forms the foundation of emotional well-being.

Spending quality time with loved ones after a demanding day rejuvenates you emotionally. It helps you emerge stronger, making it easier to face subsequent challenges with resilience.

Emotional strength permeates every aspect of your life. Start today by prioritizing your emotional health, fostering its strength, and utilizing that strength to create a life filled with happiness and fulfillment.

Your Complete Security System

Some challenges may seem deeply ingrained in history with no apparent solution in sight. However, once these challenges are conquered, they pave the way for immense success and open up new opportunities for many. Often, what appears impossible holds within it the seeds of extraordinary possibilities.

Habits serve as a comprehensive system that empowers you to leverage various methods effectively. A habit is a pattern of behavior that becomes your instinctive response to any given situation.

In the beginning, everything in the world may appear daunting. However, once you consciously engage in the process, even the most challenging tasks become remarkably achievable.

The establishment of new positive habits or the replacement of existing negative habits requires intentional and consistent practice of the desired behavior until it becomes second nature. It is through repetition and dedication that the new behavior ingrains itself as a habit.

The speed of change is directly proportional to your desire and commitment. By continuously practicing the desired new habit, you reinforce the process, allowing it to become an integral part of your daily life.

New Opportunities: New Success

During times of challenge, it is not uncommon for people to lose faith in their ability to achieve victory. However, it is your unwavering belief that can become the key to unlocking triumph. Remember, a problem only appears insurmountable until you witness someone overcoming it. If others have found solutions, so can you.

Amidst every challenge, countless success stories emerge, each one serving as an inspiration. These stories teach us not to bow down but to fight with unwavering determination. They impart a fundamental lesson of life: to adopt challenges, transforming them into opportunities and scripting our own success stories.

Challenges, in reality, are blessings in disguise. They conceal numerous hidden opportunities waiting to be discovered. Seize these opportunities and forge your path to success. There is no better time to reinvent your business and redefine your growth trajectory. The more you persevere during challenging times, the stronger you become, and this strength will sustain you throughout your entire journey.

Remember, the power to overcome challenges and adopt opportunities lies within you. With unwavering belief, resilience, and a determined spirit, you have the ability to transform adversity into triumph and create a success story that will inspire others for generations to come.

BONUS CHAPTER

"Unlock the Transformative Toolkit That Turned **Life's Challenges into Thriving Opportunities** for Countless Individuals, Redefining Their Paths to Success in Just a Few Steps!

INTRODUCING

CHALLENGES INTO OPPORTUNITIES TOOLKIT

Check more details here: **selfhelppowers.com/toolkits/**

Discover the Secrets to Overcoming Life's Toughest Trials and Crafting Your Path to Success through the "Challenges into Opportunities Toolkit."

Transform Your Life Now! Order the CHALLENGES INTO OPPORTUNITIES TOOLKIT and Gain Access to:

- Engage in a **Comprehensive Video Course** unraveling strategies to transform challenges into growth opportunities. (12 Modules):
    - Module 0: Introduction
    - Module 1: Understanding Challenges and Opportunities
    - Module 2: The Mindset Shift
    - Module 3: Identifying Your Challenges
    - Module 4: Analyzing Challenges
    - Module 5: Finding Opportunities Within Challenges
    - Module 6: Planning and Goal Setting

- Module 7: Overcoming Obstacles
- Module 8: Taking Action
- Module 9: Tracking Progress
- Module 10: Celebrating Success
- Module 11: Building Resilience for the Future
- Module 12: Quick Recap

- Access a meticulously crafted **Guidebook** offering actionable steps and insights for every hurdle you encounter.
- Gauge your strengths and areas for growth with a **Personalized Assessment Tool.**
- Set clear, achievable Professional and Personal Goals with **Goal Setting Worksheets**, guiding your journey towards success.
- Dive deep into challenges, unraveling their core and discovering pathways for resolution with **Challenge Analysis Worksheets**
- Learn the art of recognizing hidden opportunities amidst life's obstacles with **Opportunity Identification Worksheets.**
- Gain insights from **10 Real-Life Case-Studies** showcasing how challenges were turned into opportunities.
- Cultivate self-awareness and growth with **Reflection and Journaling Sheet.**
- Nurture your well-being with mindfulness practices designed for holistic growth with **Mindfulness and Self-Care Activities Book.**
- Sharpen your critical thinking with thought-provoking **Prompts for Critical Thinking worksheets.**
- Draw inspiration from **Real Success Stories and Case Studies**, mirroring your journey.

- Infuse daily motivation with a collection of **50 Powerful Quotes** to fuel your resilience.
- Access ready-to-use templates and printables for practical application and ease:
    - 30 Day Self-care Challenge Planner
    - Daily Goal Planner 1
    - Daily Goal Planner 2
    - Daily Task Planner
    - Dream Journal 1
    - Goal Setting Planner 1
    - Goal Setting Planner 2
    - Goal Tracker Planner
    - Goals to Actions Planner
    - Gratitude Journal
    - Health Tracker
    - Monthly Goal Planner
    - Project Planner
    - Reading Journal
    - Weekly Planner

You have a choice. You can continue navigating challenges as you have been, or you can begin a journey towards growth and empowerment. The "Challenges into Opportunities Toolkit" isn't just a purchase—it's a gateway to transformative experiences, propelling you towards success.

Imagine the cost of missed opportunities and prolonged setbacks compared to the value of this toolkit, empowering you to navigate challenges with finesse and resilience.

Act now to seize this opportunity for transformation. The window won't stay open indefinitely. Don't miss out on the chance to turn challenges into catalysts for your success.

P.S.: This Goal Setting program has been valued at over $1,297. However, it's now available at an introductory price of only

$67. The price will gradually increase in the coming months, so don't miss out! Grab your copy today.

Check more details here: **selfhelppowers.com/toolkits/**

ABOUT THE AUTHOR

Shaun Oliver, the luminary force behind Self Help Powers, brings over 15 years of dedicated immersion in exploring the profound depths of spiritual psychodynamics. His journey, marked by extensive study and deep introspection, led Shaun to amass a wealth of wisdom—a mosaic of insights drawn from the timeless teachings of diverse cultures and spiritual philosophies. Shaun Oliver's commitment to empowering people culminated in the creation of **SelfHelpPowers.com**—a digital haven fostering personal growth, self-discovery, and empowerment. This book stands as a testament to his mission: empowering people worldwide to unlock their potential and lead fulfilling lives. You can connect with Shaun: **info@selfhelppowers.com**

Did You Enjoy This Book? Share Your Thoughts!

Your feedback is crucial in helping this book to reach new readers.

Your positive feedback encourages others to discover the book, expanding its reach and allowing more readers to embark on this journey.

Leaving a **review** takes just a few minutes, but it makes a world of difference.

Thank you again for being a part of this story. I truly appreciate your time and engagement.

www.ingramcontent.com/pod-product-compliance
Lightning Source LLC
Chambersburg PA
CBHW050257230526
45471CB00005B/1921